The Remaking of the Church

RICHARD P. MC BRIEN

The Remaking
of the Church

An Agenda for Reform

HARPER & ROW, PUBLISHERS

New York, Evanston, San Francisco, London

Designed by C. Linda Dingler

Library of Congress Cataloging in Publication Data

McBrien, Richard P
  The remaking of the church.
  Includes bibliographical references.
    1. Church renewal—Catholic Church I. Title.
BX1746.M18   262'.001   73–6333
ISBN 0–06–065327–2

In grateful memory of
RICHARD CARDINAL CUSHING
Archbishop of Boston (1944–1970)
for his constant encouragement and support

CONTENTS

PREFACE

RICHARD P. MCBRIEN, the current President of the Catholic Theological Society of America, has written a book entitled *The Remaking of the Church: An Agenda for Reform*, which invites reflection, dialogue, and research.

A well-informed theologian, he begins with an analysis of the present malaise, attributable to the changes in the Church, by showing the influence of the theologies which underlie our discussions. The preconciliar image of the Church cannot be superimposed on the image of the conciliar Church, and the latter, in turn, squares badly with the image of the postconciliar Church which is gradually taking shape before our eyes. This point had to be made explicit, for there must be an accurate diagnosis before one prescribes remedies for illness. The weakness of the latest synod was due in part to the fact that an analysis of the concrete situation of the Church was not made in sufficient depth. Richard P. McBrien sifts out the major theological premises that confront one another at the present moment.

It must be kept in mind that at the council we, the bishops, were not always able to delve into the theological problems underlying our debates, because the council was above all pastoral in character. Furthermore, since a conciliar document must rally widespread support, it is very difficult to accentuate divergent positions. I, for one, would have gladly settled for a few less votes that were unanimous, and to have in their place some more incisive texts. A council, however, is not a theological convention, and, in any event, the Holy Spirit blows through the narrowness of our concepts and, unbeknown to ourselves and for the greater good of the Church, leads us "where, perhaps, we may not wish to go."

But all this belongs to the past, even though that past does condition the present to a very large extent. The author analyzes the situation simply to introduce what he calls "an agenda for reform." His project is an ambitious one: he touches upon a broad spectrum of theological, canonical, and pastoral problems, without, of necessity, being able to go into them at great depth, as he strives to make the Church of tomorrow more collegial, more communal, more fraternal, more human.

I shall not consider in detail each of the thirteen proposals or suggestions he puts forward. For my part, I should not subscribe to all of them, nor do I find myself in agreement with this or that judgment expressed in passing, but no one can deny that we are dealing here with problems that are important and that will have to be examined with care if we want the Church to embody in its structures and its daily life the implications of the theology which is developing in our midst. This will not take place overnight. One will have to proceed with courage—sometimes the real name for prudence—and with imagination, but above all with a lively faith in the Holy Spirit "who blows where he will," and who seems at this moment to be opening up new paths and to be entering ever more deeply into the life of his Church. There are not two churches, the one institutional, the other charismatic: There is only one Church, characterized by the interpenetration of these two aspects. For the benefit of those who might be tempted to lose heart at the sight of the mountains to be moved in an "agenda for reform," particularly in regard to the institutional aspect of the Church, it is reassuring to keep in mind that the Holy Spirit is indefectibly present in his Church through the weaknesses and gropings of men, and that he animates it from within so that the Church might find that fresh renewing breeze of the Spirit, which is none other than the initial wind, that of Pentecost.

Such is the desire expressed most recently by Paul VI in these words overflowing with hope:

This wind, this fire, this energy, this word, this richness, this interior power which is the Holy Spirit, the miracle of Pentecost, this, above all, is what the Church has need of today.

Malines, March 12, 1973 LEO-JOZEF CARDINAL SUENENS
Archbishop of
Malines–Brussels, Belgium

INTRODUCTION

My love for an institution is in proportion to my desire to reform it.
JOHN STUART MILL

THE ONGOING REFORM of human society, to which everyone is committed at least in principle, always presupposes the particular reform of society's several institutional components: universities, industries, legislative assemblies, even churches. But reform without an adequate theoretical basis is arbitrary reform and can, in the long run, work against its originally stated purposes.

Since the adjournment of the Second Vatican Council in December 1965, several projects of highly professional quality, all directed at providing a solid theoretical foundation for attitudinal and structural change in the Christian churches, have been initiated and sustained in the United States, Canada, Western Europe, and elsewhere. For obvious reasons the interest of this book is fixed primarily on developments within the Catholic Church in the United States, but it is to be hoped that the material will have a much wider application, denominationally and geographically.

Officially approved bilateral conversations have taken place among Catholics, Episcopalians, Lutherans, Methodists, Baptists, Disciples of Christ, Presbyterians, Greek Orthodox, and others, and some of these dialogues have achieved a remarkable degree of consensus on matters previously regarded as hopelessly controverted (e.g., intercommunion, the character of ordination, the authority of ecclesiastical creeds, the status of women in the Church, etc.). At the same time, the Canon Law Society of America has produced some exceptionally valuable studies, prompted by carefully planned symposia, on such matters as a bill of rights for Christians, due process for ecclesiastical personnel, broadening and making public the process for the selection of bishops, revising the relationships among executive, legislative, and judicial power in the Church, etc. These and similar studies have generally been ignored by church authorities and rank-and-file membership alike. This book will be successful if it should serve as a catalyst for bringing these studies and the fruits of the several ecumenical consultations to the attention of a larger reading public and if it should add thereby to concern about, and pressure for, constructive ecclesiastical change—concerns and pressures which have existed in varying degrees since Vatican II.

"In varying degrees," to be sure. For church reform, which was once so enthusiastically welcomed in assorted segments of the Christian community has now become "a weary business when the powers who oppose it appear without any mask, and the forces of reform have largely lost their joy and courage. The Church is becoming polarized."[1]

On the right, counter-reform measures have already begun. Efforts are made, not only to hold the level of change at its present line, but to depress that level as closely as possible to its preconciliar watermark. And on the left, Christian institutions are in the process of being abandoned altogether. Some speak of the ideal Church as one without any specific structures or location. But, as Yves Congar has observed, "Declarations of this kind are made by men who enjoy all the benefits of a solidly based Church that has allowed them their education in faith and prayer. What would things be like for the second generation that took such a proposition as its starting point?"[2]

This book addresses itself to two inextricably related issues: the theological and political conflict in contemporary Christianity, with special reference to the recent years of change in

Catholic attitudes and practice (Chapters I and II); and the determination of specific proposals for institutional change through which such conflict can constructively be resolved (Chapters III and IV). The book is an exercise in practical ecclesiology. It is concerned not only with the *why* of change, but with the *how;* not only with the mystery of the Church, but with its remaking.

RICHARD P. MCBRIEN

Boston College
Chestnut Hill, Mass.
March, 1973

The Remaking of the Church

CHAPTER I

The Passing of the Torch

"LET THE WORD go forth from this time and place, to friend and foe alike," John F. Kennedy's voice rang out in the wintry air of inauguration day, January 20, 1961, "that the torch has been passed to a new generation of Americans—born in this century, tempered by war, disciplined by a hard and bitter peace, proud of our ancient heritage.

"Let us begin anew," he continued. "All this will not be finished in the first thousand days, nor in the life of this Administration, nor even perhaps in our lifetime on this planet. But let us begin."

Lofty goals, distant frontiers, new beginnings, the passing of the torch of leadership to a younger, more disciplined generation—these were the hallmarks of liberal rebirth at the outset of the 1960s.

Just over twenty months later, at the opening of the Second Vatican Council, Pope John XXIII would confidently announce, over against the "prophets of doom" among his own advisers, that "in the present order of things, Divine Providence is leading us to a new order of human relations which, by men's own efforts and even beyond their very expectations, are directed toward the fulfillment of God's superior and inscrutable designs. And everything, even human differences, leads to the greater good of the Church."[1]

In this second case the torch of leadership had been passed to a man twice the age of the first, older even than the man the first succeeded, and yet the same spirit of hopefulness, of zest in the pursuit of unfinished business, of profound trust in the power of our individual and corporate human resources had begun to dominate the post-Pian Catholic Church just as it had begun to define post-Eisenhower America.

There was apparently little we could not now accomplish. Failure would reflect a lack of resolve, not a lack of capacity.[2]

When Karl Barth, probably the most distinguished Protestant theologian since Luther and Calvin, returned from his *ad limina* visit to Rome, at the conclusion of the council's first session, he felt compelled to announce, almost in spite of himself, that there were symptoms of a landslide taking place in Catholicism, a spiritual movement whose possibility no one had reckoned with fifty years before.

The daily enthronement of the Bible at the beginning of each conciliar meeting was more than liturgical ornamentation and Italian *bella figura.* It signaled a restoration of Sacred Scripture to the center of Catholic faith and spirituality. Pope John's opening address, Barth argued, heralded the beginning of a whole new reorganization of the Catholic Church around the demands of the gospel.

Jesus Christ, the Word made flesh, joined the inspired written Word as the focal point of concern for Catholic theology and life. There were signs of a new understanding of the relationship between divine and human freedom, between faith and its works, between Scripture and Tradition—signs which explained more fully, or which even surpassed, the long-standing doctrinal decisions of Trent and Vatican I.

Clearly there was a movement toward more active congregational involvement and participation in the service of the altar. And Catholic theologians were assuming a newly flexible stance in the interpretation of traditional dogmas of faith, once regarded as immovable obstacles not only to eventual reunion but to meaningful and productive dialogue as well.

"For a change," Protestantism's elder theoretician observed, "we *non-Roman* Christians are in a special way the ones who are *questioned.*"[3]

"How would things look if Rome (without ceasing to be Rome) were one day simply to overtake us and place us in the shadows, so far as the renewing of the church through the Word and the Spirit of the gospel is concerned?" Barth asked.[4]

Although not yet fully prepared to make that kind of generous concession, he did freely acknowledge that the stirrings of renewal in this most unlikely of places had already generated a shaking of the foundations of historic Protestantism, too long quiescent, conservative, and, yes, unreformed!

"Must not the Council . . . give us occasion to sweep away the dust before the door of our own church with a careful but nevertheless mighty broom?" he pressed.[5] "The way to unity of the Church can only be the way of her renewal. But renewal means repentance. And repentance means turning about: not the turning of those others, but one's *own* turning."[6]

The evidence supporting such judgments as these seemed to grow rather than diminish as the decade advanced, and especially as the council moved into its second, third, and final sessions.

The Catholic Church—officially, theoretically, and even at the grass-roots parochial level—began to describe itself more forcefully as a community first of all, and only secondarily and subordinately as a visible society, hierarchically structured. The "People of God" became the fundamental category of theological and pastoral self-understanding in the conciliar documents and in most of the immediately postconciliar commentaries and popularizations.[7]

From this changed perception of itself as community rather than as an institutionalized *societas perfecta,* there developed approval for, and movement toward, not only the creation of new structures designed to provide public expression for the People-of-God rhetoric (e.g., parish councils) but also the creation of new forms of spirituality (e.g., the Catholic charismatic renewal).

Indeed, as the Catholic Church's self-understanding moved

from a hierarchical/institutional model to a community/People-of-God model, so its structural organization and operation moved from a monarchical to a collegial pattern.

The Pope was no longer regarded universally as an absolute monarch. He seemed himself prepared to modify that traditional image, in style if not always in substance. Thus Paul VI made the important gesture (important in the Italian scheme of things at least) of walking in the conciliar procession at St. Peter's Basilica rather than being carried aloft according to custom. In this way he sought to demonstrate the fraternal character of his unity with the rest of the Church's bishops. He was one of them, albeit their center and head. His convoking of three international synods of bishops (1967, 1969, 1971) as a way of extending the collegial principle of church government beyond the ecumenical council itself was unprecedented in modern Catholic ecclesiastical history. His willingness on occasion to preside over, and to participate in, the synodal discussions was yet another sign of his intention to make the collegial principle work and to show his readiness, in principle at least, to yield the usual monarchical claims.

Just as the Pope himself had adopted a collegial rather than monarchical style of government, vis-à-vis the body of bishops, so the bishops themselves were called upon by Vatican II to function collegially vis-à-vis their priests (their diocesan *presbyterium*). Priests' senates were established and, in some few cases, efforts were initiated for the creation of diocesan pastoral councils, drawing laity and religious, as well as clergy, into the government of the local church.

The collegial principle required more than fraternal cooperation between Pope and bishops, or bishop and people. It also demanded application of the traditional principle of subsidiarity, central to Catholic social doctrine since the time of Pope Leo XIII. The Church was not to be regarded as a pie sliced up for administrative efficiency, but rather as a cluster of churches, each in its own way a living, self-contained expression of the Body of Christ and yet each drawing its life from the other local communities which, all together, constitute the Church Universal. Collegiality, in other words, required not only a sense of international solidarity, particularly with the Church of Rome, but also a sense of local initiative and sovereignty. Thus, the postconciliar Catholic Church was marked by occasional assertions and displays of national and regional independence. The record of the Dutch Church is a well-known example. The substantial reform movements in religious communities, especially those in the United States, were still another sign of the collegial principle at work: international solidarity without prejudice to local sovereignty.

The collegial principle, in turn, was grounded in the newly emerging conviction that the mission of the Church belongs to all its members and not simply to a few. The prevailing theology of the preconciliar era had conveniently domesticated the lay apostolate, calling it "Catholic Action," the participation of the laity in the work of the hierarchy. There had been, of course, several cynical variations of that definition, e.g., the interference of the laity in the lethargy of the hierarchy.

"Catholic Action," however, had clearly been, through the 1940s and 1950s, the dominant model for making sense of, and giving justification for, the involvement of nonordained Catholics in the life and work of their Church. The Second Vatican Council, with its insistence on the responsibility of the laity for the mission of the Church, freed the lay apostolate from its hierarchical bondage, teaching that it was a participation in the saving mission of the Church itself, a participation granted directly by the Lord himself in and through the sacraments.

Vatican II seems to have been a watershed in the declericalization of the Roman Catholic Church. Lay observers, their token number notwithstanding, were officially admitted to the council's proceedings. Laity served on various commissions and other agencies, whose composition was once uniformly clerical and religious. Halting efforts were made here and there to consult the laity in the selection of bishops and to involve them more directly, on a professional basis, in the planning and administration of parochial and diocesan educational programs.

The declericalization of the power and organization of the Catholic Church was accompanied by a corresponding declericalization of piety and spirituality. The council insisted that every member of the Church, not just priests and religious, is called to perfect holiness. There are to be no ascetical elites, no super-Christians. If the gospel is to be taken seriously at all, it is to be taken seriously by all.

The council also propelled Catholic thinking and practice in the direction of social and political responsibility. Heretofore, many Catholics were of the mind that the involvement of the Church in such activities as the American labor movement, the priest-worker movement in France, and the struggle for social justice everywhere was, at best, preliminary or peripheral to the real work of the Church; namely, the task of preaching the gospel and celebrating the sacraments. Catholics may have been visible in this or that economic or civic project (we had our "labor priests" in the 1930s and 1940s), but few were ever tempted to suggest that such an investment of time, resources, and personnel could be justified on the same theological basis as similar investments in the assorted tasks of teaching, catechesis, and worship.

Just as Catholic theology had domesticated the lay apostolate by its notion of "Catholic Action," so it had domesticated the social apostolate by its notion of "preevangelization." There were many areas into which the Church could legitimately proceed, but those of a social, political, or economic dimension could be validated only to the extent that such commitments might eventually break down the barriers of alienation and mistrust that separated the Church from those outside the Church, or, conversely, only to the extent that such engagements might tend to diminish the outflow of disaffected Catholics (especially working people) from the Church. In other words, social action was important not for its own sake, but as a means of achieving a higher end which alone belonged to the essential mission of the Church; namely, to bring outsiders into the Church where they might be exposed to the Word of God and the sacramental rites and thereby be brought more surely along the road to personal salvation, and to keep disaffected insiders inside.

The council, however, seemed to be insisting, particularly in its Pastoral Constitution on the Church in the Modern World, that the social apostolate was as much a part of the essential mission of the Church as the proclamation of the Word and the celebration of the sacraments. It severely characterized the abiding tendency to separate Christian faith from social, professional, and political attitudes and activities as "one of the more serious errors of our age."[8] The whole burden of the document was to reunite faith with action, Christian perspective with social justice.

In this regard the council was setting itself firmly in the tradition of the great papal encyclicals of the past seventy-five years: Pope Leo XIII's *Rerum Novarum* (1891), Pope Pius XI's *Quadragesimo Anno* (1931), Pope John XXIII's *Mater et Magistra* (1961) and *Pacem in Terris* (1963), as well as several official pronouncements, apart from the encyclical format, by John XXIII's predecessor, Pope Pius XII. Vatican II itself was only part of the development. There followed an encyclical by Pope Paul VI, *Populorum Progressio* (1967) and the document "Justice in the World" of the Third International Synod of Bishops (1971) wherein it was argued, directly contrary to the notion of preevangelization, that "action on behalf of justice and participation in the transformation of the world" are indeed "a constitutive dimension of the preaching of the Gospel, or, in other words, of the Church's mission for the redemption of the human race and its liberation from every oppressive situation."[9]

The accumulated wisdom of Catholic social doctrine was sufficiently impressive to warrant a word of praise from an erstwhile critic, the late Reinhold Niebuhr:

I see in modern Catholicism a great lesson for all Protestants. . . . What secularists, Protestants, and Jews don't realize is that once this Church was free, once it related itself to what we call open society and democracy, it had a greater awareness of the collective problems of justice than any Protestant, idealistic secularist, or utopian secularists ever had. . . . Now why does the Church insist on collective bargaining? Because it knows that there is a social substance in human existence and that there is a collective egoism in which you have to have a balance of power. A great deal of justice depends on an equilibrium of power between organized labor and organized management. I see this as one of the greatest achievements of modern Catholicism.[10]

The new political activism of Catholics after the council—the Berrigans, Father Groppi, and others—gives witness to the perennial sturdiness of this doctrinal tradition. Frequent Catholic complaints about "too much politics" and "not enough religion" in sermons may have been itself a sign that the papal teaching, given added impetus by Vatican II, was finally taking root. It was being communicated, with some apparent conviction, by many lower-level ecclesiastical leaders.

There were also encouraging signs of growth in the relationships between Catholicism and the rest of the Christian community. Prior to the council the Catholic Church customarily described itself as "the one, true Church of Christ." It was *the* Church. The official Catholic response to the World Council of Churches, for example, had been standoffish, even a little arrogant. Intercommunion was assumed to be impossible, apart from total conversion of "the other" to the Catholic position, and the idea of a mutual recognition of ministries was simply unthinkable. And yet with Pope John XXIII and Vatican II the Catholic Church began speaking officially of Protestants as fellow Christians and of their communities as genuine churches. We share with them, the council proudly acknowledged, our faith in Jesus Christ, our embrace of the Bible as the Word of God, our celebration of the sacraments of baptism and the Lord's Supper, our acceptance of the gospel as the core and foundation of ethical judgment and commitment. The Body of

Christ may indeed subsist in the Roman Catholic Church, but not in the Roman Catholic Church alone.

Cooperation in prayer, in social projects, in biblical translations, even in theological study were actively supported and encouraged. Pope and Patriarch in warm embrace, an Anglican archbishop preaching from a Roman Catholic pulpit, a Vatican official being courteously received at a non-Catholic ecumenical convention—scenes such as these became commonplace in the pictorial record of postconciliar Christianity. The age of mutual suspicion seemed, for the most part, to be over. Indeed, so successful had been our collective ecumenical enterprises that some would be asking, in due course, if we had already entered the postecumenical era, if we were faced now only with the task of climbing over the remains of an ecumenical movement whose work was essentially completed and of moving on toward something bigger and better.

Not many years before the Second Vatican Council the usual, and apparently official, Catholic position on Church and state and the granting of religious freedom to non-Catholic citizens followed the line that in theory the Roman Catholic Church, if it were to accede to a position of sufficient political power, would be compelled in conscience to use the state to suppress every other form of religious faith. But Catholic defenders of this hypothesis were quick to reassure their nervous audiences: we shall in all likelihood never achieve such numerical strength (our advocacy of large families and our adamant opposition to contraception notwithstanding), so the non-Catholic citizenry has nothing practical to fear. So dominant was this view that when theologians such as the late John Courtney Murray, S.J., attempted to criticize it on rigorously scholarly grounds, he was forbidden by his superiors to publish anything further on the question. Moreover, he was rudely ignored when the invitation list of *periti* was submitted for the opening session of the council, an offense corrected before the opening of the second session in September, 1963. But the "error has no rights" philosophy remained the dominant view even into the 1960s. It was an issue that would, for a time, haunt and afflict John F. Kennedy in his campaign for the American presidency.

Vatican II, adopting a position closer to Murray's than to his opponents', declared that religious freedom is based on two principles: first, human dignity requires that men not be constrained at all in making a choice so profound as the choice of faith; and, second, the act of faith itself must be free if it is to be meritorious. Thus, to impose legal restrictions on the free exercise of religion is to offend against human dignity and saving faith.

Thereafter, it would be an entirely consistent gesture on the part of the Vatican to have established a Secretariat for Non-Believers, and for that Secretariat to have acted as a co-sponsor of the First International Symposium on Belief, held in Rome in March 1969.[11] "What especially impressed the non-Catholic participants," Peter Berger, chairman of the meeting, observed, "was the atmosphere of complete freedom and openness that marked the symposium from beginning to end." It had also given to Harvey Cox "a new sense of what Rome might someday come to mean again—a place of openness and, indeed, catholicity in the literal sense of the word, a place in which all Christians and all men of good will could profoundly feel at home."[12]

Finally, the conciliar and immediately postconciliar Catholic Church seemed at last to have broken the gordian knot binding salvation and Church. It spoke less and less about itself as the "ordinary means of salvation" and of its mission as one of bringing the outsider in and of preventing the movement of the insider out. The Church would no longer identify itself *tout court* with the Kingdom of God. The council did declare that the Church is "the initial budding forth" of the Kingdom of God, but no more than that.[13] The Kingdom of God is God's— and man's—unfinished business. The whole world, including the Church, strains toward the day when all things will be brought to completion. We still live, however, in the time of the "not yet." Nothing is yet the Kingdom, not even the Church.[14]

If the Church is not yet the Kingdom of God, then the Church, like any other institution and community, is subject to criticism, from within and from without. Most of the criticism in the latter half of the 1960s seemed to come from within. The extent and intensity of Catholic reaction to Pope Paul VI's birth-control encyclical, *Humanae Vitae*, in the summer of 1968, is now a matter of historical record. It is difficult to exaggerate the significance of that reaction. The subsequent debate about papal infallibility[15] and the public criticism of ecclesiastical stagnation by Catholic theologians indicate that this trend continues.[16]

Karl Barth had spoken in 1963 of a landslide, a shaking of the foundations, a spiritual movement within Roman Catholicism. He reflected perhaps the new mood of optimism emanating from both the Vatican and Washington, D.C. In less than ten years, however, it became uncomfortably clear that both President Kennedy's and Pope John XXIII's generous impulses and assessments had been premature at best, misguided at worst.

Kennedy's new frontier would tragically include his own assassination, that of his brother, that of Martin Luther King, tumult and violence on university campuses and on city streets, accelerated traffic in drugs with corresponding increases in addiction and related crimes, right-wing backlashes on integration, social welfare, and civil liberties, the election and reelection of Richard Nixon, and, of course, the war in Indochina.

John XXIII's new order would encompass his own death the following June, widespread dissent and dissatisfaction on Catholic college and seminary campuses, unprecedented attrition of personnel within the ranks of the clergy and religious women, traditionalist backlashes against liturgical reforms and catechetical renewal, the ascendancy of repressive leadership in Roman curial posts, and, of course, Pope Paul VI's encyclical on the morality of birth control, *Humanae Vitae*.

Less than ten years after Barth's guardedly optimistic judgment about the immediate future of Roman Catholicism and about its potential impact on contemporary Protestantism, the Catholic Church is an organization marked by excessive conflict, polarization, and a debilitating drainage of human resources. Furthermore, there is now a widespread sense of frustration on the part of the rank-and-file membership, and even on the part of many bishops, with the workings of the ecclesiastical system, in which liberals and progressives had so recently placed so much trust.

Two of the root causes of this development will be discussed in the second chapter; namely, the failure of church leadership to provide the general membership with adequate reasons for change and, second, the failure of church leadership to demythologize its own self-image, in the light of contemporary theological perceptions.

These failures of leadership have, in turn, produced a sense of frustration in those who have been excluded from the decision-making process in the Church and have further undermined the membership's confidence in the quality of that leadership.

If there is to be a solution to this problem, it will necessarily involve an increase of participation in the life and mission of the Church and, therefore, some positive change in the relationship between the general membership and its leaders.

I should argue that this diagnosis and prescription, however tentatively and schematically proposed here, apply as much to the political situation as to the ecclesiastical, for I agree with those who have been insisting recently that the institutional disarray in Roman Catholicism is only symptomatic of the broader institutional malaise that now besets the human community generally and American society in particular.

Lecturers in the field of theology and related disciplines can readily identify with the observations of Senator Mike Gravel, of Alaska:

15   The Passing of the Torch

Everywhere I go, people ask the same questions: "How can we change things?" and "What can ordinary people do to beat the system?" They want to know: "Why doesn't anyone listen to us? *Really* listen, so they can find out what we want and need, not what 'they' (the entrenched establishments) say we want or think we need." Most of all, they ask: "What can I do?" or "When do *we* (the people) get a chance to run things?"[17]

The decade of the 1960s and the years beyond promised affirmative and persuasive answers to those kinds of questions. Politically and ecclesiastically it appeared as if, under enlightened leadership, the respective systems were going to work at last, that genuine participatory democracy would prosper anew. A political community so strengthened, its vision sharpened and refined, its sense of purpose elevated and refurbished, would make the most effective frontal assault on injustice, war, poverty, alienation, inadequate medical care, poor housing, shoddy education, and environmental waste that the world has witnessed in modern times. An ecclesiastical community so strengthened, *its* vision sharpened and refined, *its* sense of purpose elevated and refurbished, would become once again the most effective voice and force for the Kingdom of God and Christ on earth.

One cannot suggest, by hindsight, that Karl Barth's—or the others'—hopeful judgments about Catholic renewal and reform were somehow myopic or naïve. He reported what he saw and what he sensed. There were grounds not only for delightful surprise but for optimism as well, even enthusiasm. The torch had been passed.

CHAPTER II

The Fallen Torch

WHAT HAPPENED TO the Catholic Church after the council? Why did so many of its bright promises suddenly dim and go out? What precipitated the apparent decline and fall of the Catholic reform movement? What forces reduced that Church to the condition of "bare ruined choirs"?

Sociologists like Andrew Greeley, psychologists like Eugene Kennedy, historians like John Tracy Ellis, David O'Brien, or James Hitchcock, and journalists like Garry Wills have their own theories and they have been sharing them with their co-religionists in books, articles, and lectures over the past two or three years.[1] As far as I can determine, there has not yet been a sustained *theological* analysis of the current ecclesiastical crisis. Hans Küng and others have addressed themselves to one or another aspect of the crisis, but we still lack a comprehensive theological evaluation of the problem and its sources. This book, and this chapter in particular, is designed as a first attempt at theological diagnosis and reconstruction: What theological factors have led, in these past several years, to the unmaking of the Church, and what theological principles ought to be incorporated in any process designed to facilitate the remaking of that Church?

The problem outlined in Chapter I has its root in a theory-and-practice gap. The Catholic Church in the years preceding Vatican II was characterized by a generally constant and coherent set of practices (e.g., clericalized liturgy, monarchical government of parishes and dioceses, unilateral papal rule, and so forth). These practices flowed logically from an agreed-upon theory of the Church. Catholics did what they did and thought what they thought because there was really no viable theological alternative. This is the way Christ intended the Church to be.

At the Second Vatican Council a new set of practices were initiated and approved. Many Catholics embraced the new practices for extrinsic reasons alone (i.e., out of a spirit of obedience to the Pope or to the ecumenical council), but without any interior conversion of mind and heart. In other words, they willingly accepted new practices, and the elimination or substantial modification of some older practices, without any corresponding change in their theoretical outlook. On the contrary, they held fast to the old theory while trying desperately to accommodate to the new practices.

To this point the crisis precipitated by the theory-and-practice gap was relatively manageable. One's conscience after all has a certain measure of flexibility, and a pragmatic spirit had never been completely foreign to the Catholic mind. However, the new set of practices promoted by Vatican II and by various other concomitant influences were not to remain stable. It would not be enough for some Catholic parishioners to have a parish council as a new consultative agency within a local Christian community. They would want more than a rubber-stamp relationship to pastoral policy-making. Pressure was to be applied to make such councils canonically deliberative, and not merely consultative, bodies. In other words, they were to be, in fact and in law, the decision-making agency of a given community, with the pastor (or bishop, in the case of diocesan pastoral councils) in the role of president, but without the power of absolute veto. Nor would it be enough for ecumenically minded Catholics to gather on Thanksgiving morning for a common prayer service with their Protestant neighbors and friends, or for festivity and fellowship during the week of prayer for Church unity every January. They would sense a deeper oneness with many of their non-Catholic brothers and sisters, not only as human beings but as Christians. They would grow in the conviction that they and their non-Catholic counterparts were sufficiently one in faith to permit, even to demand, a common celebration of the Eucharist. And so the process would continue: from a generally moderate set of reforms generated by Vatican II to a more imaginative and pastorally experimental set of reforms generated by the postconciliar mood and spirit dominating influential segments of the Church.

It was difficult enough for traditional Catholics to have tolerated and grudgingly accepted the conciliar reforms while holding fast, for the most part, to the theological assumptions of the preconciliar period. But the postconciliar reforms tested the Catholic pragmatic spirit beyond its point of endurance. The Catholic who still understood the Church in preconciliar categories was faced with four options: (1) to leave the Catholic Church, recognizing that, for all practical purposes, the Catholic Church no longer exists; (2) to pretend to agree that these newest, more radical changes could be justified theologically and then to accede to them; (3) to try and hold the line at about the same point to which the conciliar teachings had brought the Catholic Church by late 1965; or (4) to commit oneself totally to the task of reversing even the conciliar trend and of restoring the practices of the Catholic Church to their preconciliar status.

The first option is unthinkable for Catholics of a right-of-center orientation. They continue to envision the Church as their single link with God. The impact of the ecumenical movement notwithstanding, they regard "the one, true Church" as their "ordinary means of salvation."

The second option is almost equally unpalatable. Flexing one's conscience is one thing, breaking it in half is another. They do not see how a Church which Christ apparently founded as a monarchical institution of salvation can delegate its authority to people who have no divine right to it. Thus, the election of bishops, a restricting of the present canonical power of the Pope, recognizing the validity of Protestant ordinations and sacraments, cannot be taken as legitimate accommodations; they are outright compromises with the truth and, as such, are acts of infidelity to the Lord.

The third option is clearly more acceptable than the first two, but even here the course of events seems to make it increasingly unrealistic. It is apparent by now that Catholic reformers will never be content with the modest reforms of Vatican II. Moreover, many reformers have already left the Church (for them the first option is always viable) because of their sense of frustration with the slow pace of change. Indeed, the theologians' statement to which I referred in the preceding chapter was composed and circulated precisely to counteract this obvious growth of pessimism and discouragement among the Church's progressive groups. It seems, therefore, that the conciliar changes embodied within themselves the ingredients for continual change. That is to say, once a change in the traditional set of practices has been accepted, one has already accepted the principle of endless, unchecked change.

For many traditional Catholics the fourth option is really the only viable one. The theological and spiritual schizophrenia required of them after the council—doing things they really didn't believe in or saw any point to—could no longer be sustained. They yearn rather for the "good old days" before the council, not necessarily because they enjoyed the Latin Mass or clerical control or ecclesiastical isolationism, but because in those "good old days" they at least had reasons for everything they did and for everything that was, in effect, done to them and for them. There was no theory-and-practice gap, and there were no schizophrenics.

And here, of course, we have the elements of real conflict, leading almost inevitably to a state of polarization—a Church of armed camps, suspiciously facing one another across a kind of DMZ heavy with the smell of recrimination, sarcasm, ridicule, and anger. The Catholic on the traditionalist side insists, now that he is down to his last option, on a return of the Church to its preconciliar status: a ban on intercommunion of any kind and under any circumstance; the shepherding of religious women back into convents, distinctive garb, traditional apostolates, and monarchically administered discipline; a complete pullback from social and political involvement; the replacement of all catechetical textbooks and other materials with the Baltimore Catechism or its equivalent; the restoration of the cult of the Pope. Evidence of such retrenchment at a time when many other Catholics are convinced that things are moving too slowly and that the very credibility of the Church is at stake produces the most virulent kind of counter-reaction. Rightwing extremism generates a proportionately acute form of leftwing extremism. And then the process reverses itself, spewing forth, in turn, a spiral of accelerating extremism. Meanwhile, somewhere in the middle, moderately liberal and moderately conservative elements struggle to hold the Church together while moving it gently—the one element a little more rapidly than the other—toward progressive reform and consolidation of change. To the extremist, however, every moderate is an extremist of the opposite view. The moderate liberal is regarded as an extreme rightist by the extreme leftist, and as an extreme leftist by the extreme rightist. And the moderate conservative appears as an extreme leftist to the extreme rightist, and as an extreme rightist to the extreme leftist. Indeed, the moderates are sometimes more sharply vilified by the extremists than are the extremists of the opposite side. The moderate is regarded as a hypocrite, a traitor to the cause, the most dangerous of enemies because of his appearance of moderation and balance.

As I acknowledged earlier in this chapter, there are sociological, psychological, historical, and political reasons for this crisis, and analyses developed out of these particular disciplines have begun to appear. I have suggested, however, that the crisis still requires some kind of sustained theological analysis. I have identified the theological problem with the gap between theory and practice which has existed in the Catholic Church since 1965, and which continues to exist. (I do not suggest, of course, that such a gap exists only there, but my point of reference throughout this book must be the Catholic experience. I should hope, however, that my analysis of that experience will be applicable to a wider segment of the Christian community.)

Changes were initiated without providing adequate justification. Too many Catholics acquiesced in the changes without the advantage of sound reasons. Other Catholics, at the opposite end of the spectrum, demonstrated such enthusiasm for change that they even pressed from time to time for irresponsible change. They, too, were hampered by a deficiency of theory.

Change without reason is arbitrary change. People, inside or outside religious organizations and communities, cannot tolerate arbitrary change for long. It produces a schizophrenia of the soul. Ecclesiastical leaders were at fault for not preparing the membership of the Church for the changes specifically adopted by Vatican II and, even more importantly, for not preparing the membership for the many changes implicitly endorsed by the council. One reason for the leadership's failure is its historic separation from the community it serves, a separation produced by a mythology of the episcopal and papal offices which not only explains but even seems to require this separation. Leadership without accountability; decision-making by the few, for the many. Several theological solutions to these problems will be outlined in some detail in the third chapter. The remainder of this second chapter will be devoted to a fuller analysis of the roots of the problem; namely, a careful description of the theory-and-practice gap to which I have been alluding heretofore.

The problem can be schematized in the following way (see Glossary, p. 167, for definitions of terms):

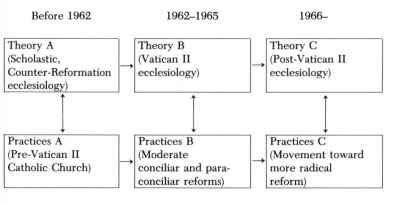

Before 1962	1962–1965	1966–
Theory A (Scholastic, Counter-Reformation ecclesiology)	Theory B (Vatican II ecclesiology)	Theory C (Post-Vatican II ecclesiology)
Practices A (Pre-Vatican II Catholic Church)	Practices B (Moderate conciliar and para-conciliar reforms)	Practices C (Movement toward more radical reform)

Practices A

The Catholic Church before the Second Vatican Council was a readily distinguishable entity—identifiable in customs, in habits, in styles of life, in organizational structure and operation. It was a Church of remarkable unity (perhaps, more accurately, "uniformity"), without apparent internal trouble or crisis. The Catholic community of the 1940s and 1950s was a relatively peaceful one because, in my judgment, the various practices which constituted pre-Vatican II Catholicism were validated, each in its own way, by an underlying theory of Church. Catholics acted the way they acted, and thought the way they thought, because this was clearly the way they were supposed to act and to think, by the will of Christ himself—or so they were convinced.

The pre-Vatican II Catholic Church was a Church without parish councils or diocesan pastoral councils. It was a Church without priests' senates or international synods of bishops. It was a Church where religious women ("nuns" in those days) were dressing, living, and functioning in a reassuringly predictable manner—in habits, in convents, and in conventional ecclesiastical apostolates. It was a Church, indeed, where women, not just religious women, were without voice or vote.

In the pre-Vatican II Catholic Church priests and religious were regarded as having attained a higher form of Christian life; the laity, especially those who married, had somehow followed an easier course, taking what the Church offered as a "lawful remedy for concupiscence." In every debate about the relative merits of virginity (celibacy) and the married state, no Catholic could reasonably argue in favor of the latter, at least not in the face of so much evidence presumably supplied by St. Paul and the Council of Trent. When the laity involved themselves, however peripherally, in the life and work of their Church, their involvement was always perceived not as a direct participation in the mission of the Church, but rather as a participation in the mission of the hierarchy (Catholic Action).

In the pre-Vatican II Catholic Church, collaboration and cooperation with Protestants and other non-Catholics was generally considered as risky, and even tenuously orthodox, behavior. There were no common prayer services, no ecumenical marriage ceremonies. Catholics understood that attendance at non-Catholic services *(communicatio in sacris)* was always forbidden, except in extraordinary circumstances (e.g., the funeral of a relative). But even in those rarely acceptable cases, the Catholic could not contribute more than bodily presence: no singing, no utterance of prayers, no reading of Scripture, no reception of the putative sacramental elements. The pre-Vatican II Catholic attitude toward non-Catholic worship was even more severe than that. Not only were Catholics discouraged from attendance at heretical worship, they were also taught that, were the political situation more favorable, the Catholic Church would be required in conscience to suppress all forms of non-Catholic worship and religious life—on the indisputable premise that "error has no rights." I have already suggested, in the first chapter, how this position proved to be a temporarily serious obstacle in John F. Kennedy's climb to the presidency of the United States in 1960.

The liturgical isolation carried over into the realm of academic life as well. Catholics studied Protestant thought second and third hand. To read the erroneous doctrines first hand would violate the moral dictates of the Index of Forbidden Books. If Catholics, particularly Catholic seminarians, did not read Protestant authors, *a fortiori* they did not take Protestant courses. Indeed, Catholics were not even allowed to use any versions of the Scripture except those specifically approved by ecclesiastical authority. The so-called "common Bible" was as yet only an idea in a pioneer's head.

The Catholic Church before 1962 was a Church of selective political involvement. Catholicism had its "labor priests" in the 1940s and 1950s, just as France had its "priest-workers," but no one was prepared to argue that these apostolates were anything more than specialized, extraordinary and, therefore, expendable ministries. The Church's professional personnel might legitimately apply themselves to one or another area of the social and political order, for the sake of economic justice or human rights, but such application of resources could be justified only if the Church could satisfy itself that the Church's missionary position would be improved thereby. In other words, if the Church's official presence in the socio-political arena could break down the barriers between nonbeliever and Catholic or, on the other hand, could dissuade Catholics from abandoning the faith of their fathers, then such allocation of resources and personnel could be approved as a bona fide preparation for the real missionary work of the Church. Such a commitment was considered to be a part of the process of "preevangelization."

The preconciliar Catholic Church was an organization largely controlled by the assumption that its leadership and its policies were immune from serious criticism by its own membership and that its structures and operations were immune from substantial internal reform. The Church was, after all, the Body of Christ, without spot or wrinkle. To impute incompetence to its leadership was to impute bad judgment to the Holy Spirit, to Christ, and to Christ's Vicar on earth, the Pope. To challenge its policies was to challenge the promise of Christ to be with the Church all days, even unto the consummation of the world. To argue on behalf of institutional reform was simply to revert to Protestantism.

The liturgy in its latinate mold was another durable characteristic of the pre-Vatican II Catholic experience. Before the liturgical movement finally won its victory (of sorts), the Mass occupied an extraordinarily ambivalent place in the Church. On the one hand, it was universally acknowledged to be the sacrifice of Christ and the most important sacred action the Church could herself perform; on the other hand, the Mass ritual remained for many Catholics an incomprehensible drama: a rite, however complicated, to produce hosts for the tabernacle. The Eucharist so thoroughly embodied a whole cluster of interrelated beliefs that, when the Mass's intricate choreography was altered, the belief system changed with it.

This pre-Vatican II Church highly prized papal statements, whether in encyclicals, allocutions, decrees, even casual reflections prepared for specialized groups of pilgrims. No one considered it strange that a new magazine should have been given the title, *The Pope Speaks,* nor that many intra-Catholic debates about social and political policy should have relied so heavily on papal pronouncements, going even to the point where one party would attempt to trick the other into unwittingly disagreeing with the Pope, by quoting something from an encyclical, on behalf of one's own argument, without disclosing the source. The assumption—which liberals and conservatives alike accepted—abounded that to disagree with the Pope was to be, well, wrong.

The mystique surrounding the papal office was such that no Catholic would have questioned the process by which their own local leadership was selected. The Pope alone had to make that decision, although he could seek prudent counsel from his curia, certain important bishops of the country in question, and from his nuncio or apostolic delegate. But the choice was his, and ultimately the Holy Spirit's. As the Vicar of Christ, the Pope's decision was simply the human mechanism through which the Spirit chose to work.

There were few priests leaving the ministry in the days before the council, and the few who did leave were sharply branded: "fallen-aways," "lapsed priests," "shepherds in the mist." To leave the priesthood was to leave the Church (for it carried with it the penalty of excommunication) and to leave the Church was to turn away from salvation itself. For those who strayed from the path, there was always Confession. Indeed, Confession may have been the one structural element that held all the other assorted practices together. The confessional provided a way of dealing with uncertainties and qualms on the part of the membership, of overcoming what psychoanalysts call "resistance." "Whatever happens," Peter Berger noted, "the believer must be prevented from what we have called 'alternating'—that is, prevented from an ecstasy or conversion which will transport him outside the system, even for a moment of intellectual inspection."[2] I intend now to outline the theological content of that system.

Theory A

The most sophisticated and academically serious preconciliar exposition of the mystery of the Church is available in the so-called "Spanish Summa" *(Sacrae Theologiae Summa),*[3] a seminary textbook once widely in use throughout the Western Catholic world. The author of the tract on the Church *(De Ecclesia),* Joachim Salaverri, S.J., divided his material into three sections: the social constitution on the Church, the teaching authority of the Church, and the supernatural nature and properties of the Church. If one agrees that placement is the first and fundamental act of interpretation, then one should see that Salaverri already betrayed an exceedingly hierarchical and institutionalized understanding of the Church. According to his systematic presentation, the Church is principally a visible society, hierarchically structured. Apparently the most telling thing that one can, and ought, to say about the Church is that Jesus intended it to be a public, external means and sign of salvation (unlike the Protestant vision which, according to the usual caricature, perceives the Church as an invisible, spiritualized community without the requisite appurtenances of law and order). Jesus conferred upon the leaders of the Church the threefold power of teaching, ruling, and sanctifying. This authority is to be exercised according to a politically monarchical pattern. Presumably, the role of the nonordained is *to be* taught, *to be* ruled, and *to be* sanctified. Of the three duties of papal and episcopal leadership, the most important seems to be teaching. On the basis of his analysis of these structural and official elements, he concludes that the Roman Catholic Church is "the one, true Church of Christ."[4]

The second of only three sections, or "books," in the Salaverri system is devoted exclusively to this teaching authority, or magisterium. Here he insists upon that teaching's immunity from error (infallibility), whether in the case of the Pope alone or in the case of the bishops in union with the Pope. The First Vatican Council, however, very carefully restricted the use of the charism of infallibility: the Pope had to be speaking as supreme head of the Church *(ex cathedra)*, on a matter of faith and morals, and with the clear intention of binding the whole Church. Since the definition of papal infallibility in 1870, only once did a Pope exercise that prerogative: in defining the dogma of the Assumption of the Blessed Virgin. One could hardly conclude that Vatican I's dogmatic decision had much real practical impact on the cognitive life of the Catholic Church, so it was not totally surprising that theologians and others in the Church should have been tempted to extend Vatican I's infallibility dogma to other teaching situations not explicitly covered by the original definition, e.g., papal encyclicals. Theologians insisted that, even though other papal declarations might not strictly fulfill the conditions precisely established by Vatican I, these other pronouncements, by reason of their supremely authoritative source, were to be regarded "as if" they were immune from error, i.e., "for all practical purposes." Thus, Salaverri and others argued that teachings promulgated through the ordinary magisterium (e.g., encyclicals, decrees of curial congregations, etc.) were to be received with an internal and religious assent of the mind *(mentis assensus internus et religiosus).*[5] Practically, this meant that no one, not even a theologian, could publicly oppose such pronouncements, and that nonspecialists could not even *think* negative thoughts about these pronouncements, without violating the requirements of filial loyalty and piety.

The third book of the *De Ecclesia* tract seems, on the surface, to move the discussion from a highly legalistic plane to a level that is at once more biblical and theological. Such is not really the case. Even in the treatment of the supernatural character of the Church (i.e., its concern for salvation), Salaverri shapes the material along essentially institutional lines. The second thesis in the section discloses the really controlling premise: "The Church is a perfect and absolutely independent society, with full legislative, judicial, and coercive power."[6] When he speaks of the Church as the Body of Christ, a rich Pauline image, he does so, once again, in fundamentally legalistic terms: how one enters the Body of Christ (by baptism) and how one is excluded (by heresy, apostasy, schism, or excommunication).[7] The material on the four notes of the Church (one, holy, catholic, and apostolic) is also drawn in accordance with apologetical considerations: the Catholic Church *alone* is one, holy, catholic, and apostolic; no other church can make that claim; and so forth.[8]

It should be remembered that the Spanish Summa's presentation was the most sophisticated and academically serious in this

preconciliar period. There were other, less critically preten-
tious, presentations which were circulated in equivalently un-
critical ways: in catechisms and religious instruction classes,
from pulpits and mothers' knees. The practices described in the
preceding section flowed, by force of inner logic, from the theory outlined above, and from that theory's several corollaries.

Thus, there were no parish or diocesan councils because bishops are, by the will of Christ, monarchs in their own dioceses,
while pastors somehow share in that monarchical authority of
the bishop, at least by some vaguely understood principle of
analogy. In any event, the Church was established by Christ as
a monarchical institution, and councils of any kind, including
even priests' senates, would violate the Church's divine constitution. There could be no thought of international synods of
bishops because the Pope, again by the will of Christ, rules as
an absolute monarch. Indeed, so firmly fixed was this notion of
absolute papal supremacy that there were some theologians
before Vatican II who seriously argued that there was no longer
any need for ecumenical councils. Vatican I had to be the last.

It made sense, according to Theory A, for nuns to remain in
convents, in distinctive religious garb, and in clearly discernible
ecclesiastical apostolates because the order of the sacred is
sharply distinguished from the order of the secular; furthermore, women are, by the will of God, subordinate to men, in the
Church as well as in society.

Priests and religious, moreover, are called to a higher form of
Christian life. Ordination and religious profession elevate the
recipient to a status of spiritual superiority. The laity, on the
other hand, are called to a more modest style of Christian expression. They are not really expected to strive for perfect
holiness. Their more passive involvement in the life and work
of the Church is a necessary consequence of their secondary,
dependent status in the Christian community. To the extent
that the laity participate in the mission of the Church, they do
so by way of hierarchical delegation, because the hierarchy

alone has directly received the mission of teaching, ruling, and sanctifying. Where the bishops find themselves incapable of fulfilling that mission by themselves, Christ allows them to solicit assistance from those who are not directly called but who, in extraordinary circumstances, can legitimately enter the breach on a temporary, standby basis.

There was little political commitment, other than the occasional engagement of priests in labor-management affairs, because political, social, and economic questions were regarded as having nothing essential to do with the work of the Church. The mission of the Church is the communication of salvation. It does this by preaching, teaching, catechizing, and administering sacraments. All else is peripheral at best. It can be validated only to the extent that the Church can satisfy itself that such activities may break down the remaining barriers between Church and nonbelievers or, conversely, may slow the outflow of disenchanted Catholics. The social apostolate is not part of the core of evangelization, it is rather something to be done *before,* or parallel to, the real work of preaching the Gospel. It is *pre*-evangelization. Is it really surprising that the majority of American Catholics, in a 1968 Gallup poll, admitted that they were troubled by the increasing involvement of their Church in social and political areas? What does this activity have to do with religion, after all? So severe was this dichotomy between Christian faith and social action in the early 1960s that Vatican II would characterize the gap-mentality as "one of the more serious errors of our age."[9]

The generally unfavorable attitude toward Protestants in the pre-Vatican II Catholic Church cannot be explained simply as bad grace on the part of Catholics. Catholics were not, and presumably are not, any more unpleasant or close-minded than various other groups in modern society. Their theoretical convictions about the meaning and purpose of the Church, however, made it difficult, if not impossible, for them to perceive the Protestant more sympathetically than they actually did.

The Catholic Church alone was founded by Jesus Christ. The Protestant churches began much later in history. Charts and graphs easily demonstrated this. The deficiency of the Protestant churches was not a matter of opinion, but of historical record. Because the Protestant communities broke away from the "one, true Church of Christ," they severed themselves also from valid ministry and valid sacraments. Thus, attending Protestant worship services had to be out of the question. Nothing salvific could happen there. Furthermore, active participation might convey the impression that one accepted the authority and legitimacy of the presiding minister and the ecclesiastical organization which he represented. That, too, was inconceivable. While Catholics could, and ought, to be neighborly and kind toward their non-Catholic acquaintances and friends, there was a point beyond which the Catholic could not proceed. Indeed, if it ever were to happen that the Catholic community acquired sufficient political strength in a given country, even in democratic lands, Catholics would be bound in conscience to suppress all forms of non-Catholic faith and worship. Non-Catholics in the United States were quickly "reassured," however, that such a development was highly unlikely. But principle was still principle, and "error has no rights."

In the preconciliar Catholic Church radical self-criticism, or indeed criticism even of a milder strain, was simply not part of the empirical landscape. Why not? Because the conventional theology of the Church held that the Church was already the Kingdom of God on earth. To criticize the Church is to criticize the Kingdom, which is to criticize God himself. As Salaverri had argued at the end of his own *De Ecclesia* tract, the Catholic Church is alone the Church of Christ because it is *already* holy. Perhaps no element in the pre-Vatican II ecclesiology had more serious practical consequences than this commonly accepted judgment that Church and Kingdom are identifiable. The "triumphalism" which was so roundly attacked by several bishops at the council emerges directly from this central theological assumption. If the Church is the official arena of God's redemptive presence and activity, then no one can responsibly argue that such a Church is in need of substantial reform, in head, in members, or in structures. And the keys of the Kingdom are unchallengeably in the hands of the Pope. When Rome speaks, the cause is finished: *Roma locuta est, causa finita est.*

In the pre-1962 Catholic Church, it was not taken as a sign of weakness that the liturgy remained a generally foreign and, therefore, incomprehensible experience for many of her members. The sacraments, it was argued, work *ex opere operato,* i.e., when the rite is celebrated according to the norms set down by the Church, the recipient can be assured that the grace of Christ is infallibly available to him if only he is properly disposed to receive that grace. The Church, too, is a kind of sacrament. One need not understand everything it does nor be pleased with everything it requires, but one nevertheless understands that behind the façade lies the reality of the Lord. Whether or not one appreciates the Church's policies and demands, one knows that he is in touch with Christ and, therefore, on the way to salvation. The sacraments are given to the Church to ensure the passage of her members from this world to eternal life. They are means of grace. Their intelligibility is entirely secondary to their efficacy. That is why the liturgical movement received so little enthusiastic response from so many Catholics. They really did not see the point of it.

A key theoretical element in preconciliar Catholicism is the concept of apostolic succession. The common theological interpretation of that concept held that the sacramental and jurisdictional legitimacy of Catholic bishops is grounded in their historical linkage with the apostles themselves. The Catholic hierarchy is apostolic in character because Catholic bishops alone can trace their sacred orders back, in an unbroken line, to the time of the primitive Church. Once again, so the argument goes, charts and graphs based on historical record, not theological opinion, reveal evidence that is conclusive and irrefutable. Thus, bishops cannot be selected by a democratic process. Their mandate and their authority come from God, not from the people, just as the mandate and the authority of the apostles were derived from God, not from the early Christian community. The Pope stands in the place of Peter as the head of the college of bishops. As the one to whom Christ gave the power of the keys, Peter—and his successors—has the right and the duty to select those who are to share that power with him.

No organization, of course, can achieve its goals if its middle-management personnel are alienated from the higher, policy-making leadership or are ineffective in the performance of their duties. Priests, particularly those functioning in parishes, exercise such middle-management authority in the Church. Serious disaffection and attrition in their ranks would severely hamper the operation of the total organization.

The attrition problem was controlled, however, by the theology of the indelible character imposed by ordination: "once a priest, always a priest." Those priests who withdrew their hand from the plow and turned back did so under pain of excommunication and, therefore, jeopardized their eternal salvation. The Church is the ordinary means of salvation, the Kingdom of God on earth. To disengage oneself from the Church by violating one of her most serious disciplinary prescriptions is to depart from the way of salvation. Outside the Church, it was assumed, there is no salvation, the qualifications of the Father Leonard Feeney case notwithstanding.[10] And if one regarded the Church as the ordinary means of salvation, then one logically had to regard the sacrament of Penance as the ordinary means of forgiveness from sin. Protestants and others could beg God's pardon, but they could never have the absolute assurance that God had heard them and had blotted out their guilt. Catholics, on the other hand, received both pardon and peace, *ex opere operato*.

The disaffection problem was less manageable from a theoretical point of view. It was often proposed, in subtle and sometimes in explicit ways, that the rank and file in the Church owed their superiors unquestioning loyalty and obedience. The fragile texture of this notion, so universally agreeable to those holding higher authority, became unmistakably apparent in the latter half of the 1960s, under the impact of the Second Vatican Council, to which we now turn our attention.

Practices B

During the four or five decades preceding the Second Vatican Council—beginning with the pioneering work of Dom Lambert Beauduin, Virgil Michel, O.S.B., and others, encompassing the formation and early organizational flourishing of the North American Liturgical Conference, and culminating in Pope Pius XII's encyclical *Mediator Dei* (1947)—the dominant progressive force in Roman Catholicism was clearly the liturgical movement. Its closest competitors in terms of influence and effectiveness were the social action and biblical movements.

The really distinguishing mark of a liberal Catholic in the pre-Vatican II period, however, was his interest and involvement in the sacramental apostolate. This commitment led many, in turn, to social action as the practical application of the liturgy, and to biblical studies as the historical and theoretical underpinning of the liturgy. But liturgy remained the focal point; the others were subordinate to it.

Accordingly, it should not have been surprising to anyone who had been aware of this long-term trend in twentieth-century Catholicism that liturgical renewal and reform should have provided the forces for change their real breakthrough at the council. The Constitution on the Sacred Liturgy was the first major document approved by the council (December 4, 1963) and it was the clearest initial indication that the earlier progressive rumblings at the opening session the previous year had some substance behind them. These were not the customary rhetorical trumpetings of the liberals. The movement was so securely rooted that it could bear fruit in a hard documentary way. Once the apparent preserve of peripheral, odd-sort Catholics, liturgy and the sacramental apostolate were now endorsed at the Church's highest authoritative level. The Mass and the other sacred rituals entered a period of rapid sequential change. The dialogue Mass, already in use here and there on a trial basis before the council, became more standard fare. The congregation was expected now to give at least the simple responses: *Et cum spiritu tuo; Deo gratias; Amen.* Vernacular singing was encouraged at key moments in the Mass: the offertory, for example. There were efforts to introduce congregational participation without sacrificing the ancient Gregorian chants. In some parishes, relatively rare indeed, the laity sang the *Kyrie, Sanctus,* and *Agnus Dei,* and fewer still attempted the *Gloria* and *Credo.*

But many Catholics were to miss the real point of liturgical renewal. It was directed not only at wider congregational participation but, more importantly, at deeper congregational understanding. It was not enough that the people were singing or giving some of the Latin responses. They had to know what they were doing, and why, when they gathered for Mass.

Commentators, first the ordained, then the nonordained, appeared in the pulpits to help the laity make the transition from one part of the Mass to another. The Epistle and Gospel were read in English as the priest, with his back still to the people, read both passages in Latin, in a low, barely audible voice.

Finally, some of the prayers of the Mass went directly into the vernacular, with the rule of thumb that those parts directed at the people and designed to elicit a response from them were put into English, while those parts meant only for the celebrant were left in Latin. Changes of this sort, involving a gradual, and sometimes haphazard, movement from Latin to the vernacular, were nightmarish for publishers of altar missals. The liturgy was becoming a looseleaf affair and the Catholic religious books business went crashing through the floor.

The next stages followed quickly upon these. The altar itself —in most churches built solidly into the back wall, an ornate and utterly immovable mass of marble and stone—was turned around to face the people. In most cases, however, temporary altars (simple tables covered with white cloth) were placed out into the sanctuary, about halfway between the old altar—whose tabernacle became its last, relevant link with the liturgy—and the Communion rail. This proved to be one of the most controversial of all changes, with opposition almost uniformly clerical. The priest must have his back to the people, it was argued, not because he is indifferent to them, but because he is their leader. He leads them toward God; they follow—behind him, as in a parade.

The Mass went entirely into the vernacular; offertory processions were introduced; Communion was received standing rather than kneeling; the altar facing the people became the norm rather than the exception; and the laity answered all the prayers which had been originally theirs from the earliest centuries. The "mystery," the disenchanted complained, was gone. The Mass was there, right out in the open, for everyone to see and to touch. How could anyone continue to believe that something sacred was being transacted between God and man when the rites themselves had become so, well, intelligible, and when ordinary mortals (unlike the anointed priests) now had so much to do with it?

The conciliar Church carried its new liturgical understanding of community over into areas of ecclesiastical government. Plans were laid, by conciliar directive, for the formation of national episcopal conferences, priests' senates, and diocesan synods—all designed to provide structural substance to documentary injunctions.

Parish councils were mandated for the first time, and the mechanism for their gestation and birth was put in motion. The same held true, although at a much slower pace, for diocesan pastoral councils. Sisters' leadership conferences made their initial appearance, as the first stirrings of feminism osmotically penetrated the Catholic shell. Other groups such as the National Association of Laity were formed. The forces of change entered the world of communications as well: the *National Catholic Reporter* would significantly alter the character of American Catholic life and thought in the mid-1960s.

Vatican II's inauguration of the age of the laity was not without its unpleasant side effects. The council's exaltation of the lay state in general and of marriage in particular set many priests wondering whether their own personal sacrifices had really been worthwhile after all. Was celibacy truly the better part? If laymen were now to be encouraged to take a more active role in the liturgy and even in the decision-making process of Church life, what could be the point to a special priestly caste? The resignation of priests from the active ministry would accelerate to an organizationally dangerous degree in the postconciliar years, particularly after the well-publicized departure of Charles Davis in England during the Christmas holidays of 1966, but the groundwork was already being laid here in these conciliar years.

Catholics and other Christians began displaying a greater social awareness and activism even during the conciliar years; and the civil rights movement, more perhaps than the peace movement which had not yet taken recognizable shape, was clearly the point around which this renewed interest in *diakonia* (service) coalesced. I should expect that history will italicize the role of Martin Luther King, Jr., in steering the Catholic Church, as well as many of the other churches, toward a more political and prophetic style of mission. It was King who reminded American Christians of their individual and corporate responsibility to shout a defiant "No!" now and again to governments and other institutional forces. It was King who attracted priests, ministers, nuns, and laity alike to Selma, Alabama, in 1965, for the marches and demonstrations that were to mark the turning point in the black struggle for equal opportunity and equal rights under the law. Having been schooled already in the art of mass protest and having shed their assorted cultural and theological inhibitions, priests and sisters would find it a short and relatively easy step from the civil rights movement to the peace movement. The way was prepared and made straight for the subsequent Berrigan phenomenon which would so transform the character and image of postconciliar Catholicism.

Just as the common calamity of the Second World War had generated a sense of urgency for the cause of Christian unity in the Western world, so the collaborative experience of the civil rights movement—and the still powerfully residual influence of Pope John XXIII himself—helped American Christians put their denominational differences in an entirely new focus. Indeed, the Vatican II years set in motion almost as many ecumenical changes as liturgical: the week of prayer for Christian unity was now celebrated together; official observers were invited to the conciliar sessions and encouraged to speak their minds—even Paul Blanshard had been received with some warmth in Rome; Catholic observers, in turn, finally accepted longstanding invitations to the various meetings of the World Council of Churches, and the Pope himself visited Geneva; and, finally, the preparations were made for the initiation of formal, bilateral conversations between theologians and ecclesiastical leaders on such matters as the development of dogma, baptism, the Eucharist, the ordained ministry, and even the papacy. The first of such meetings, involving Catholics and Lutherans, on the one hand, and Catholics and Presbyterians, on the other, were held even before the council had finally adjourned (March 1965 and July 1965, respectively).

The Pope and other Catholic leaders were determined, however, to show that their ecumenical outreach extended even beyond the confines of the Body of Christ. On May 17, 1964 Pope Paul VI established a new secretariat for the development of relations with non-Christian religions. In his first major encyclical, *Ecclesiam Suam,* the Pope insisted that dialogue must occur not only between Catholics and non-Catholic Christians but between Catholics and non-Christians and even between Catholics and those without any religious faith at all. Catholics were directed by their leaders to take another look at traditional catechetical attitudes toward Jews in particular, and to clean up the textbook rhetoric which remained in conflict with the new conciliar teaching and spirit. Dialogue with Marxists shattered still other precedents. Pope John XXIII had initiated the process by his widely publicized gesture of receiving in audience the son-in-law of Soviet Premier Khrushchev, and from there the interaction moved quickly to theological and diplomatic levels. The Christian-Marxist dialogue gave birth, on the Christian side, to a new "theology of hope" and, on the Marxist side, according to some political commentators, to the uprising in Czechoslovakia. In any event, the old Ottaviani-Connell-Fenton position on Church and state, which had been the dominant "orthodox" view in the United States and throughout the Catholic world generally until the council, was now in full retreat. John Courtney Murray, S.J., at long last was being vindicated in his views.

When the council opened in September 1962, John Kennedy was still in the White House and American universities, cities, and other institutions were slumbering in relative peace. By the time the council closed in December 1965, Kennedy had been assassinated, Lyndon Johnson had been elected president by one of the great landslides in American history, the military buildup in Vietnam had reached ominous proportions, universities were in a state of veritable siege, and summer was becoming the acceptable season for urban riots. Challenges were now being mounted against the several powerful institutions of modern society, and the Church would not remain immune. On the other hand, by present standards of ecclesiastical self-criticism, the situation during the conciliar years would have to be described as mild and restrained. One of the first challenges to traditional ways of doing things in the Church had been raised a year before the council by Hans Küng in his best-selling book, *The Council, Reform, and Reunion:* "Renewal and reform of the Church are permanently necessary because the Church consists, first, of human beings, and, secondly, of sinful human beings."[11] It is difficult indeed to exaggerate the influence which that one book exercised throughout the Catholic Church in the early 1960s. Küng articulated openly what many Catholics had evidently believed but had been unable or reluctant to express so directly and unambiguously. Küng's work was not without precedent. Eleven years earlier the eminent French ecclesiologist, Yves Congar, O.P., had completed a historically solid study of the problems and prospects of ecclesiastical reform in *Vraie et fausse réforme dans l'Église*, but by order of the Vatican the book was withdrawn almost immediately from circulation.[12] Of course, nowhere were the Church's institutions and customs criticized more forcefully, or indeed more publicly, than in the council chamber itself. The three-pronged attack by Bishop DeSmedt of Belgium against the spirit of triumphalism, legalism, and clericalism embodied in the first draft of the council's Constitution on the Church was one of several instances.[13] But not until after the council ended did the self-criticism become universal. The turning point came exactly one year later with the departure of Charles Davis and his widely circulated attack upon Catholic doctrine, theology, and practice.

Theory B

For those Catholics still locked into Theory A, the changes in practice outlined in the preceding section were simply without intrinsic warrant. "Intrinsic" is the key word here. These Catholics had accepted the changes in the first place only because of their *extrinsic* validation by the Pope, the ecumenical council, and—less enthusiastically—the local bishop and their pastor. The failure of local leadership to communicate the *intrinsic* reasons for the changes is perhaps the greatest single cause of the excessive conflict and polarization that followed. The Catholic laity were relegated to a kind of schizophrenic isolation: thinking one way, acting in another, and utterly alone in their confusion.

The theoretical basis for these changes is contained principally, although not exclusively, in the documents of the Second Vatican Council—"not exclusively" because the documents themselves are products of theological currents which were already at work. The conciliar phenomenon itself is inexplicable apart from these deeper, antecedent currents.

I have already outlined the major elements of the conciliar theology in the first chapter in order to underscore the spirit of high promise that permeated the Catholic Church on the eve of its apparent institutional collapse. Herein I shall correlate the conciliar teaching with two elements: Theory A as proposed in the Salaverri textbook, and Practices B insofar as they follow upon and reflect the conciliar teaching.

1. *Comparison of Theory A and Theory B:* The first point of contrast between Theories A and B is their respective organization of theological material. Structuring is always the primary and fundamental act of interpretation. The Baltimore Catechism, once so widely in use throughout the American Catholic Church, serves as a good example of how this principle works. The catechetical material is divided into three major sections: the Creed, the Commandments, and the Sacraments. Thus the Christian life essentially requires belief in certain revealed truths proposed in the doctrinal formulations of the Church; second, it requires that certain activities be performed or avoided in order to demonstrate the Christian's fidelity to the saving doctrines; finally, the Christian is given certain aids by the Lord to make it possible to believe those truths and to remain faithful to their ethical implications. The placement of the sacraments at the end of the total schema is already an act of theological interpretation. The sacraments are thereby per-

ceived as the tools to do the job whose essential dimensions (Creed and Commandments) have already been outlined fully. On the other hand, if the section on the sacraments had been placed first rather than third in the catechetical plan, it would have been necessary to rewire completely the catechism's whole theological network. Coming in the first place, the sacraments would have been portrayed as mysteries of God's presence and as models of Christian community and action, rather than as means of grace and aids to salvation. This would have required, in turn, a revision of our understanding of the place of creedal formulations and ethical imperatives in Christian experience and mission.

The Salaverri synthesis, summarized earlier in this chapter, labors under similar structural difficulties. In organizing the theological data on the Church, Salaverri implies that institutional and structural questions are of first importance. The Church, it would appear, is principally a social institution with a hierarchical structure, and that structure is monarchical in character. The institution exists to deliver salvation, which is itself given as a reward for right belief and right action. The final norm for the rightness of belief and action is the teaching authority of the Church, vested primarily in the Pope, but also in the Pope and the bishops together.

Vatican II's organization of its ecclesiological material is considerably different from Salaverri's. The Church is first and foremost a mystery, in the Pauline and Augustinian sense. It is the public, historical sign of God's invisible, redemptive presence to the world and to mankind. This is the most fundamental truth about the Church: God is therein present to the world; the Church is "a kind of sacrament."[14] Sacraments, according to traditional Catholic doctrine, are both signs of faith and causes of grace. Indeed, they cause what they signify. They are efficacious signs. Thus, when the council taught that the Church is "a sign of intimate union with God, and of the unity of all mankind," it was compelled by the force of its own doctrinal logic to conclude that the Church is "also an instrument for the achievement of such union and unity."[15]

Every "mystery" has two aspects: visible and invisible. The invisible aspect is always God; the visible aspect changes. Christians believe, for example, that God is present in the human flesh of Jesus Christ, or in the consecrated eucharistic elements of bread and wine, or even in the person of their neighbor. To call the Church a mystery is to affirm that God is somehow present within it. That accounts for the invisible element. Where or what is the visible element of that invisible presence? The council taught that the divine presence is externalized through the people who constitute the Church. God is present to the Church in and through the community itself. Accordingly, the second chapter in the council's Dogmatic Constitution on the Church speaks of the community as "The People of God." It is not until the third chapter that the document raises the question of structure and authority. As many undoubtedly recall, the council engaged in sustained debate over the placement of chapters two and three: Should the chapter on the People of God precede or follow the chapter on the hierarchy? In the earlier drafts the chapter on the hierarchy had preceded the chapter on the People of God. It was argued, however, that this sequence only perpetuated the notion that the Church is principally an institutional reality, with an elite corps of episcopally consecrated members, rather than a community called forth by God to embody the presence, and carry on the work, of Christ and his Spirit. The argument prevailed and the chapters were reversed. Had the meaning of this relatively simple and straightforward decision ever been communicated effectively, much of the Church's subsequent turmoil might have been averted. The significance of that decision is clear: the Salaverri framework was no longer the criterion; it had been set aside. The Church is not primarily a hierarchical institution or a perfect society; it is primarily a community, a pilgrim people still laboring in imperfection. Responsibility for the mission of the Church is no longer to be conceived as the exclusive prerogative of the hierarchy; it is a responsibility, rather, whose dimensions are universal, applying equally to laity, religious, and clergy, all of whom are joined together in a multiplicity of pluriform ministries in the service of the one mission.

Second, whereas Salaverri is remarkably silent about the social mission of the Church, beyond the official, authentic proclamation of the Word and the valid, authoritative celebration of the sacraments, the council acknowledges in its Pastoral Constitution on the Church in the Modern World that the Church must be concerned that "this world might be fashioned anew according to God's design and reach its fulfillment."[16] Her conviction is that "she can contribute greatly toward making the family of man and its history more human."[17]

Third, Salaverri's insistence on the uniqueness of Catholicism to the ecclesial detriment of other Christian communities is in contrast with the council's speaking of these Christian bodies as "churches,"[18] and its reminding of the Catholic community that these non-Catholic Christians have indeed the "right to be honored by the title of Christian, and (to be) properly regarded as brothers in the Lord. . . ."[19] Salaverri had grounded his argument for uniqueness on the traditional four notes, proposing that the Catholic Church alone is *already* one, holy, catholic, and apostolic. The council, on the other hand, acknowledged that these qualities were not yet within the full possession of the Church. Thus the Church embraces sinners in her bosom and, therefore, "is at the same time holy and always in need of being purified."[20] There is an important methodological principle implied here; namely, that all of the notes are to be understood dialectically and eschatologically, i.e., they are, in one sense, already realized and, in another sense, not yet realized. Only at the end of history will they be brought to perfection.[21]

2. *The connection between Theory B and Practices B:* The liturgical changes, although regarded by many Catholics, including clergy, as arbitrary, unnecessary, and upsetting to faith,

had perhaps the deepest roots of all the changes which had been initiated or promoted by the council. It has long been accepted as a basic principle of sacramental theology, articulated by St. Thomas Aquinas and doctrinally defined by the Council of Trent, that sacraments cause grace precisely insofar as they signify that grace. Indeed, sacraments are both signs of faith and causes of grace. "Because they are signs," Vatican II declared, "they also instruct." If the sign is unintelligible, the signified reality is closed off. "It is therefore of capital importance that the faithful easily understand the sacramental signs. . . ."[22]

It is not enough, consequently, that the rituals be performed according to precise rubrical detail. If the liturgy is "to produce its full effect, it is necessary that the faithful come to it with proper dispositions. . . . Pastors of souls must therefore realize that, when the liturgy is celebrated, more is required than the mere observance of the laws governing valid and licit celebration. It is their duty also to ensure that the faithful take part knowingly, actively, and fruitfully."[23] It is for this reason that the "Church earnestly desires that all the faithful be led to that full, conscious, and active participation in liturgical celebrations which is demanded by the very nature of the liturgy. Such participation by the Christian people as 'a chosen race, a royal priesthood, a holy nation, a purchased people' (1 Pet. 2:9; cf. 2:4–5)," the council concluded, "is their right and duty by reason of their baptism."[24]

When initiating a change in the external forms of Christian worship, the Church can have only one primary goal: the "full and active participation by all the people."[25] Texts and rites are to be modified in order that the people can "understand them with ease and . . . take part in them fully, actively, and as befits a community."[26]

It is this element of community which provides the broadest theological base for the liturgical changes. The people assemble for worship, not as individuals, but as members of Christ's Body, indeed as members of one another in Christ. Unlike moments of private prayer and devotion, the sacraments, and especially the Eucharist, are meant to signify and realize the unity of the Church. The reality of the Church is fully engaged in every celebration of the Eucharist. The Church is the community of Jesus' disciples; the Eucharist is that community's sacrificial meal of fellowship and thanksgiving. It is a community engaged in community worship.

An understanding of the Church that is chiefly organizational and hierarchical and of the sacraments that is chiefly mechanistic and individualistic can neither explain nor assimilate the kind of liturgical change which Vatican II promoted. If every baptized Christian is not called to missionary responsibility, then every baptized Christian is not called to liturgical responsibility. If the mission of the Church has in fact been given to the few, for the sake of the many, then so, too, is the power and duty of worship given to the few, for the sake of the many. And so forth.

Over against Theory A, the Second Vatican Council taught that the Church is primarily a mystery, not a hierarchical institution or a perfect society, and that the external side of the mystery is the community itself, not its hierarchy or its doctrines. This holy people—laity, religious, and clergy alike— shares in the prophetic, priestly, and kingly ministries of Christ.[27] There is a common bond uniting the priesthood of the ordained and the priesthood of the nonordained: "Each of them in its own special way is a participation in the one priesthood of Christ. . . . For their part, the faithful join in the offering of the Eucharist by virtue of their royal priesthood."[28]

Five or ten years earlier, an individual theologian or catechetical writer expressing such views as these would have been dismissed as a "Protestant" or a "heretic." Today those Catholics whose understanding of the Church and its sacraments remains fixed on Theory A continue to make the same kind of charge against theologians, catechists, and others who, in much more agreeable circumstances, disseminate exactly those views, but now not only in their own name and with the limited authority of their own scholarship, but with the approbation and support of an ecumenical council.

The seminal development of national episcopal conferences, priests' senates, and similar groups was also entirely consistent with the conciliar ecclesiology. Vatican II did not teach, as the manuals clearly had, that the Church is, by the will of Christ, a monarchical institution, with the Pope at the top of the ecclesiastical pyramid, and each bishop at the summit of a subsidiary, diocesan pyramid. This view had been widely inferred and circulated soon after the premature closing of the First Vatican Council in 1870. That earlier council had vigorously endorsed the concept of papal primacy and of papal infallibility, but time ran out before it could turn its attention, as it had planned, to the problem of the episcopacy and other ministries within the Church. Consequently, a seriously distorted, because truncated, view of ecclesiastical government and authority gained much support. The First Vatican Council had been a triumph for the papalist party in the Church and of the Pope personally over against his several political and religious detractors. But other contemporaries saw immediately the problem inherent in the unfinished condition of the conciliar pronouncements. Cardinal Newman, for example, had counseled his friends, in the face of their grave disappointment and concern, that the next council would correct what Vatican I had just done, but he and his associates waited in vain. It was not until the Second Vatican Council, ninety-five years later, that the Catholic Church attempted to restore the theological and canonical balance between papal and nonpapal authority. The council's achievement is incorporated in its central, although not completely unambivalent, doctrine of collegiality.

One of Theory A's central assumptions was that the Pope alone exercises supreme and full authority in the Church, that the bishops were somehow his helpers rather than genuine collaborators in the governance of the universal community. The council, however, taught that "the episcopal order is the subject of supreme and full power over the universal Church,"[29] although never apart from the Pope.

Theory A had made it appear that bishops were only the delegates or surrogates of the Pope in their local dioceses, that the Pope alone had direct and immediate authority not only over the whole Church but over each local community as well. The council declared, over against that view, that the bishops are not "to be regarded as vicars of the Roman Pontiff, for they exercise an authority which is proper to them. . . ."[30]

Theory A had argued that bishops receive their episcopal authority by an act of Pope in which their properly episcopal jurisdiction is conferred. On the contrary, Vatican II insisted, "one is constituted a member of the episcopal body by virtue of sacramental consecration and by hierarchical communion with the head and members of the body."[31]

Theory A had conveyed the impression that the division of the Church Universal into hundreds and thousands of local churches (parishes, dioceses) was dictated principally by administrative need. The Pope alone is responsible for the governing of the whole Church, but he is manifestly incapable of doing it without assistance. The Church is divided into smaller, more manageable segments, and representatives of the one, absolute monarch are appointed to supervise those segments. These overseers, called "bishops," are responsible directly to the Pope, although his personal diplomatic intermediary, an apostolic delegate or nuncio, may act in his place in order to facilitate prompt and efficient communication. Vatican II, on the other hand, taught that the Church is itself a community of local churches. Its unity is the result of a building-up, rather than breaking-down, process. The Church Universal is the international cluster of local churches: "In and from such individual churches there comes into being the one and only Catholic Church. For this reason each individual bishop represents his own church, but all of them together in union with the Pope represent the entire Church joined in the bond of peace, love, and unity."[32]

The Body of Christ is present in each local community, and these local communities together constitute the Church Universal. "This Church of Christ," the council declared, "is truly present in all legitimate local congregations of the faithful which, united with their pastors, are themselves called churches in the New Testament."[33]

Theory A had understood the episcopal-presbyteral relationship in the same manner as it had conceived the papal-episcopal relationship; namely, priests at the parish level are merely the delegates or representatives of the bishop. Although the emphasis is not so strong here as in the papal-episcopal paradigm, the council nonetheless seems to have been proposing that bishops are related to their priests as the Pope is related to the other bishops. The relationship is collegial, and the style of government, therefore, must be collegial. Priests "constitute one priesthood with their bishop."[34]

Accordingly, the development of national episcopal conferences follows upon the theological and doctrinal principle that bishops must be in collegial union not only with the Pope but also with one another, because the Church Universal is the community of all these local congregations. The relationship of an individual bishop and his diocese, on the one hand, and the Church of Rome, on the other, cannot be conceived as unilateral and vertical (between bishop/diocese and Pope/Rome), but multilateral and both vertical and horizontal (between bishop/diocese and Pope/Rome, and also between bishop/diocese and all other bishops/dioceses). A regional or national structuring of this collegial unity seems to be a legitimate and reasonable application of the fundamental principle. The same would hold true for the formation of priests' senates. If the bishop and his priests in a given community constitute one priesthood, one presbyterate, then their sacerdotal unity in the governance of a local church ought to find some structural realization which would not only manifest their unity in an institutional way but also provide the institutional elements to fulfill their common missionary responsibility. It is not a situation of over-against-ness, because priests are not over against bishops, nor are bishops over against the Pope. All of them are bound together in a collegial union.

The initial development of parish councils and diocesan pastoral councils, just as the previous development of national episcopal conferences and priests' senates, followed upon particular directives and fundamental theological principles embodied in the documents of the council. The mission of the Church belongs to all of its members, not just to the episcopally ordained and those whom they specifically designate to share in their missionary responsibility. Everything which the council said about the Church as People of God it explicitly applied on an equal basis to laity, religious, and clergy.[35] Those with pastoral authority cannot conclude that they alone have been given the missionary mandate from the Lord. Rather, "it is their noble duty so to shepherd the faithful and recognize their services and charismatic gifts that all according to their proper roles may cooperate in this common undertaking with one heart."[36] Against the common view that the laity share only indirectly and derivatively in the work of the Church, the council declared: "The lay apostolate, however, is a participation in the saving mission of the Church itself." Such participation is not communicated, as it was once uniformly assumed, by legal or canonical delegation. On the contrary, it is "through their baptism and confirmation" that all Christians "are commissioned to that apostolate by the Lord Himself."[37] And, finally, over against the view that within the community of the laity women are inherently inferior to men in the exercise of the apostolate, the council condemned discrimination based on sex,[38] and argued that women must participate more widely not only in the apostolate of the Church,[39] but also in the cultural life of the world at large.[40] On the basis of such teachings, it would be difficult indeed to suggest that parish councils or increased ecclesiastical activism on the part of women, and especially religious women, are somehow without theological or doctrinal foundation. The given practices follow upon, and are validated by, given theories.

The new emphasis on lay spirituality and the dignity of marriage may have had the unfortunate side effect of creating an identity crisis within the ranks of the Church's clergy, but the emphasis, and the practices following from it, is also securely grounded in the conciliar documents and in contemporary theology. The "whole Church" is called to holiness, because all are called—laity, religious, and clergy alike—to fulfill the Church's mission. If the Church is called to be a sacrament of Christ, then each of its members is called to signify Christ's presence in the world. They can do this only to the extent that they possess the fruits of the Spirit: mercy, kindness, humility, meekness, patience. "Thus it is evident," the council concludes, "that all the faithful of Christ of whatever rank or status are called to the fullness of the Christian life and to the perfection of charity."[41] Holiness is incarnate, not abstract. A Christian is not conformed to Christ in a generalized way, but always in terms of his or her particular situation in life and in the Church. Thus the insistence on the universality of Christ's call to holiness, over against the view that the ordained or religiously professed alone are summoned to the perfection of Christian virtue, is given without prejudice to the importance and distinctiveness of priestly and other forms of Christian ministry. Priests are bound to attain sanctity "in a manner proper to them" in the sincere and tireless exercise of their offices.[42]

The new social activism on the part of Christians, particularly priests, ministers, and sisters, is similarly rooted in an explicitly formulated theory of Church and mission. The Church, like Jesus, must give itself "so that this world might be fashioned anew according to God's design and reach its fulfillment."[43] It must offer to mankind "honest assistance . . . in fostering that brotherhood of all men which corresponds to this destiny of theirs."[44] The Church has a solitary goal: to carry forward the work of Christ under the lead of the Spirit, "to give witness to the truth, to rescue and not to sit in judgment, to serve and not to be served."[45]

"In fidelity to conscience," the council continues, "Christians are joined with the rest of men in the search for truth, and for the genuine solution to the numerous problems which arise in the life of individuals and from social relationships."[46] To those engaged in struggles of this kind, the council issues a reminder that the Lord has given us his assurance "that the way of love lies open to all men and that the effort to establish a universal brotherhood is not a hopeless one."[47] It is true, of course, that earthly progress, in a social, political, or economic sense cannot be identified simply with the growth of God's Kingdom. There is no need now to repeat the mistakes of nineteenth-century Liberalism and some of the less grievous errors of the Social Gospel movement of the early twentieth century. Nevertheless, to the extent that earthly progress can contribute to the better ordering of human society, "it is of vital concern to the Kingdom of God."[48] The elements of such earthly progress are "human dignity, brotherhood and freedom, and indeed all the good fruits of our nature and enterprise"; it is a Kingdom of "truth and life, holiness and grace, of justice, love, and peace."[49] Because the council believes that the Church "can contribute greatly toward making the family of man and its history more human,"[50] Vatican II argues that the present split "between the faith that many profess and their daily lives deserves to be counted among the more serious errors of our age."[51] The Old Testament prophets called this split scandalous and Jesus himself threatened it with grave punishments. "Therefore, let there be no false opposition between professional and social activities on the one part, and religious life on the other. The Christian who neglects his temporal duties neglects his duties toward his neighbor and even God, and jeopardizes his eternal salvation."[52]

The new spirit of cooperation with, and respect for, Christians separated from the Catholic community is also consistent with the theory of Church proposed by the Second Vatican Council. There are more than Catholics in the Body of Christ because it is the sacrament of baptism, and the faith which it signifies, which establishes the fundamental bond of communion with Christ: "all those justified by faith through baptism are incorporated into Christ . . . [and] therefore have a right to be honored by the title of Christian."[53] Even beyond the sacrament of baptism, there are many elements which unite Catholic with non-Catholic Christian in a clear, though uneven, bond of communion: "the written word of God; the life of grace; faith, hope, and charity, along with other interior gifts of the Holy Spirit. . . ."[54] These other communities, which can be called even "churches," have their place in the mystery of salvation as instruments of the Spirit of Christ. Furthermore, "whatever is wrought by the grace of the Holy Spirit in the hearts of our separated brethren can contribute to our own edification."[55]

If these principles are true, then it follows that "we must come to understand the outlook of our separated brethren. . . . Of great value for this purpose are meetings between the two sides, especially for discussion of theological problems, where each can deal with the other on an equal footing."[56] For the same reason instruction in sacred theology and related disciplines must reflect an ecumenical perspective. At the same time Catholics must remember that the manner of expressing their beliefs can be an obstacle to dialogue. Furthermore, not all truths are of equal value and importance. "There exists an order or 'hierarchy' of truths, since they vary in their relationship to the foundation of the Christian faith."[57]

The way to unity is also facilitated through cooperation in social and political matters, whereby the features of Christ the Servant are set in greater relief and each Christian community can more easily learn "how they can understand one another better and esteem one another more, and how the road to the unity of Christians may be made smooth."[58] In any event, we are never to impose any burden, for the sake of Church unity, beyond what is indispensable (Acts 15:28).[59]

The new concern for non-Christians and even for dialogue with Marxists is rooted in two convictions: (1) all mankind, Christians and non-Christians alike, are called to the Kingdom of God; people of every religious faith are committed, with symbolic variations, to be sure, to the coming of this Kingdom;[60] and (2) all mankind, including now atheists and other nonreligious peoples as well, are responsible for, and should be concerned about, "the rightful betterment of this world in which all alike live. Such an ideal cannot be realized, however, apart from sincere and prudent dialogue."[61] Consequently, "the Catholic Church rejects nothing which is true and holy in these [other] religions. She looks with sincere respect upon those ways of conduct and of life . . . [which] often reflect a ray of that Truth which enlightens all men."[62] She therefore exhorts her members to enter into dialogue with the followers of other religions and to collaborate with them in promoting those spiritual and moral values which are common to them all.

The generally more tolerant attitude of the Catholic Church toward non-Catholic Christians and non-Christians is rooted, in turn, in two theological principles: the dignity of the human person and the freedom of the act of faith.[63] On these two pillars rest the council's declarations concerning religious freedom:

This freedom means that all men are to be immune from coercion on the part of individuals or of social groups and of any human power, in such wise that in matters religious no one is to be forced to act in a manner contrary to his own beliefs. Nor is anyone to be restrained from acting in accordance with his own beliefs, whether privately or publicly, whether alone or in association with others, within due limits.[64]

The newly critical attitude toward the Church, evident for example in Küng's first book, *The Council, Reform, and Reunion,* is also grounded upon a specific theoretical base: the Church is subordinate to the Kingdom of God, and it is not identical with it.[65] Since the Church is not yet the Kingdom, it embraces "sinners in her bosom" and is therefore "at the same time holy and always in need of being purified, and incessantly pursues the path of penance and renewal."[66] This tendency to make Church and Kingdom coextensive was perhaps the most serious theological deficiency of Theory A. If the Church is already the Kingdom, it is beyond all need for reform and renewal of any kind. The council taught, however, that while the Church clearly exists for the sake of the Kingdom of God (this is indeed its "single intention"),[67] the Church is no more than the "initial budding forth of that Kingdom,"[68] and then only to the extent that it manifests the presence of Christ through its corporate holiness.[69] This more modest evaluation of the Church-Kingdom relationship proved to be the crucial element in moving contemporary Catholic thought from Theory B to Theory C.

NEXUS

The period of greatest change in modern Catholic practice has been occurring since the adjournment of Vatican II in December 1965. The real source of the excessive conflict in contemporary Roman Catholicism is here. If there had been no further movement beyond Practices B or Theory B, those still addicted to Theory A could have managed somehow. But the process of change continued on both levels.

The relatively conservative, carefully regulated liturgical changes endorsed by the council were resisted at first by traditionalist Catholics, particularly the clergy, and then by progressive Catholics, particularly the laity. The changes that were regarded as "too much and too ineffective" for one side were regarded as "too little and too ineffective" for the other.[70] Neither side would win a victory. Some additional changes were mandated: a signal to the right-wing that their worst fears about continued, unchecked change were correct, and a source of frustration to the left-wing because of the consistently timid and slow-paced character of such change. Both sides, as it happened, decided to seize the initiative from the papal-episcopal-curial corps. The traditionalists, convinced now that the conciliar "reforms" (Practices B) were a Trojan horse, began their efforts to restore Catholic life to its preconciliar vigor. A return of the Latin-English Mass (half a loaf being better than none) was one of their goals, and in 1972 they achieved it.[71] The progressive, convinced now that the conciliar changes were simply a liberalized face-lifting of preconciliar Catholicism, decided to adopt a much freer attitude toward ecclesiastical protocol and disciplinary decrees. They promoted liturgies in small groups, with spontaneous prayers, flexibility in structure, dispensation from formal liturgical vestments, dialogues instead of homilies, nonordained presiding officers, communication by non-Catholics, and so forth. The current polarization of the Catholic Church is constituted and stimulated principally by the tug-of-war between these two extremist forces.

Practices C

The rapid growth of the Catholic charismatic movement since its informal inception at Pittsburgh's Duquesne University in 1967 provides some measure of the dissatisfaction of many Catholics with the routinized character of the conciliar changes, especially in matters liturgical.[72] These Catholics insist that there are important implications in the conciliar teaching which the council itself failed to perceive. The conciliar changes (Practices B) did not go so far as certain elements of the conciliar theology (Theory B) radically required, particularly its understanding of the Church as a community, of the Eucharist as the central experience of Christian community, of the Holy Spirit as the source and ground of community, and of the lay apostolate as the instrument of the Spirit in the larger human community. The new emphasis on smaller, more diversified kinds of community within religious orders is another indication of how the conciliar theology has made an impact on postconciliar Catholicism in a way undoubtedly unforeseen by many of the conciliar fathers.

The sustained popularity of the writings, tapes, and lectures of Father Eugene Kennedy, M.M., professor of psychology at Loyola University in Chicago, is a mini-phenomenon in itself. Kennedy has consistently italicized the Church's responsibility to serve its members as a context for personal, human growth —a place where the values of freedom, honesty, trust, individuality, and so forth, are held in highest regard, really as well as notionally. To this day books on the dynamics of personal growth through community involvement continue to outpace more strictly academic volumes. Catholic best-seller lists are headed by such titles as Kennedy's *The Pain of Being Human* and Dr. Thomas Harris' *I'm O.K., You're O.K.*

A movement from Practices B to Practices C is also evident at organizational levels: the regular convening of international synods of bishops since 1967; the establishment of the National Federation of Priests' Councils and of the Leadership Conference of Religious Women; the introduction of due process in the government of the Church; formal interdisciplinary studies into the matter of selecting bishops, with the specific intent of legitimizing a widening of that selection process to include laity, religious, and clergy; the public criticism of Pope Paul VI's encyclical *Humanae Vitae* in the summer of 1968; the debate about papal infallibility initiated in large part by the appearance of Hans Küng's *Infallible? An Inquiry* in 1970; the ongoing, publicized contestation between Rome and the Church in Holland.

Efforts have also been made to shift the balance of power in existing ecclesiastical organizations, e.g., parish councils and priests' senates, to make them deliberative as well as consultative bodies, invested with corporate decision-making power. In some few dioceses team ministry models have been adopted in parishes to replace the traditional monarchical-feudal model for pastor-curate relationships. In several Protestant churches women are now being admitted to ordination and pressure is being applied within the Catholic Church to allow women to become priests. A study commission of the American Catholic bishops has already endorsed the principle of ordaining women to the diaconate.

As I suggested earlier in this chapter, no single postconciliar event had more immediate effect than Charles Davis' decision in December 1966 to resign from the priesthood and to leave the Catholic Church. A whole new attitude toward priestly celibacy in particular and about ministerial life-styles in general followed directly upon that action of Davis'. A Society of Priests for a Free Ministry has been formed to seek constructive pastoral solutions for the thousands of married priests who have been separated canonically from the priesthood. Some Catholics have urged the Church's leadership to retain the services of priests who do marry. Heavily financed studies of the American Catholic priesthood tend to reinforce the common judgment that priests themselves no longer accept the traditional patterns of ministerial behavior and are in favor of much wider options, particularly as these might apply to the selection of leadership and the style of its exercise.

The civil rights activism of the early 1960s blended smoothly into the activism of the peace movement in the later 1960s. Berriganism changed the profile of contemporary American Catholicism as surely as any other single factor. The election of Father Robert F. Drinan, S.J., to the House of Representatives of the United States in the fall of 1970 raised anew the question whether or not priests ought to be in elective politics.

Under the auspices of the American Catholic Bishops' Committee on Ecumenical and Interreligious Affairs and of the corresponding agencies of the other Christian churches, bilateral theological conversations were conducted throughout the United States, beginning in 1965, on such basic doctrinal questions as the Nicene Creed, baptism, the Eucharist, the papacy, the priesthood, and dogmatic development. At the same time pressure increased for some Eucharistic sharing between Catholics and other Christians and also for the mutual recognition of their respective ministries. Not surprisingly, in the absence of any flexibility on the part of the designated official leadership, canonically unauthorized instances of intercommunion have been increasing steadily since the council.

The Canon Law Society of America's present liberal, progressive image is itself a sign of the profundity of the changes which have continued to occur since the council's adjournment. The society has been responsible for reforms in the handling of marriage cases, has secured the adoption of due process by the American bishops, and has come to the legal defense of Catholics in difficulty with church authorities, e.g., the case of the Washington, D.C., priests suspended by Cardinal O'Boyle in the aftermath of the *Humanae Vitae* controversy. This latter gesture is of the highest significance. In the recent past canon lawyers were generally perceived (and indeed they perceived themselves) as the direct employees and servants of the ecclesiastical leadership, after the fashion of corporation lawyers. Now, however, the canonists see themselves at the service of the whole Church: bishops, priests, religious, and laity alike. It is a change in posture which Theory A Catholics, particularly ex-canonist bishops, cannot understand or accept. When they use phrases such as "in the service of the Church," they really mean "in the service of the hierarchy." They identify Church with hierarchy, just as they identify Church with Kingdom of God and Body of Christ with Roman Catholic Church.

If anyone needed proof that something had changed in the life of the Catholic Church following the council, the new wave of ecclesiastical self-criticism amply provided it. Charles Davis wrote in 1967 that he had experienced the Church "as a zone of untruth, pervaded by a disregard for truth."[73] Thirty-four Catholic theologians who, unlike Davis, have remained in the Church, outlined some of the major problems of ecclesiastical life in similarly direct terms:

> Widespread complaints are being raised in various parts of the church: the appointment of bishops in secret without the cooperation of clergy and people concerned; a lack of openness in the process of decision making; repeated appeals to one's own authority and to the duty of others to obey; insufficient motivation of ecclesiastical claims and directives; an authoritarian style of government that neglects genuine collegiality; a patronizing attitude toward laity and priests who are unable to have recourse against the decisions of the hierarchy.[74]

Not even these theologians, however, have dared to go so far as Father Andrew Greeley, who characterized the American Catholic bishops as "morally, intellectually, and religiously bankrupt,"[75] nor has the rhetoric of these theologians ever approached the sharpness of Philip Berrigan's characterization of the Church as "a whore."[76]

For preconciliar, Theory A Catholics, these recent trends in liturgy, ecumenism, social activism, democratization, and self-criticism are doctrinally unorthodox. For Theory B Catholics with a strict constructionist's view of Vatican II's teaching, these recent trends are abuses based on illegitimate extensions of the conciliar pronouncements. Accordingly, Theory B Catholics make every effort, in the name of moderation and good order, to contain the process of practical change within the pastoral, theological, and attitudinal range (Practices B) already outlined earlier in this chapter; and Theory A Catholics, sensing the futility of holding the line at Practices B, with which they were never comfortable in the first place, push for a restoration of the old order as outlined already at the beginning of this chapter (Practices A). To complicate the problem further: there are also some Practices C Catholics who lack an underlying theology to explain and sustain their new style of Catholic life. They are simply reacting against their own Theory A formation and Practices A experiences, without really having grasped the significance of the conciliar transition. Meanwhile, those who have in fact advanced theoretically from A, through B, to C, and who therefore recognize the weaknesses as well as the strengths of Practices B, are frustrated almost to the breaking-point by the mounting evidence of a practical regression from B to A: the restoration of the Latin-English Mass; stubborn support for traditional life-styles for religious women (Consortium Perfectae Caritatis); the use of episcopal authority to set theological (and not just doctrinal) guidelines for Christian education; the informal, secretive blacklisting of theologians, catechists, psychologists, sociologists, and others; the continued appointment of conservative-to-traditionalist, safe bishops; the retreat of the Church to the condition of a political eunuch (e.g., the ready acceptance of White House invitations to conduct worship services or lead a political convention in prayer); the new toughness applied to priests who wish to resign from the active ministry; and so forth.

We have here the makings of polarization.

Theory C

I should argue that Theory C is fundamentally a development from Theory B, in a way that Theory B is *not* a development from Theory A. "The real seeds of a new outlook . . . [had] been sown in the field of the Church," as Karl Rahner observed.[77] There is some continuity, of course, in the movement from A to B, but in several specific instances, as we have already seen, there are real changes, involving a rejection or an amendment of a conventional position. Theory C, on the other hand, recognizes that, at certain key points, Theory A continues to inform Theory B principles. In one sense, Theory C is Theory B, shorn of its ambivalences.

The following are examples of this ambivalence in Vatican II: while the council taught that the Church is the whole People of God, it also insisted that Christ rules that Church through the Supreme Pontiff and the bishops, and full incorporation into the Church requires the acceptance of the "entire system" and union with "her visible structure."[78] Collegiality could be, and is, interpreted by some to mean only that the Pope ought to consult the bishops when it is convenient, but meanwhile he retains full and supreme governing authority over the whole Church.[79] The council emphasized the apostolate of the laity, religious, and lower clergy, but these apostolates are always subject to, and are carried on at the pleasure of, the hierarchy and ultimately the Pope. The council may have cast a kinder eye upon non-Catholic Christians, but it continued to insist that those who know that the Catholic Church was made necessary by God through Jesus Christ and yet who would refuse to join her or to remain in her cannot be saved.[80] Despite the insistence upon the Church's service to the world, the council also acknowledged that the Church has no proper mission in the political, economic, and social order. Her purpose, rather, is a religious one.[81]

How are we to resolve these apparent inconsistencies? (1) Did the council intend to take away with the right hand what it had already given with its left? (2) Was the council even aware at the time that what it was saying in one document tended to differ from what it had already said in another, or indeed that what it was saying in one part of a document tended to differ from what it had already said in another part of the same document? (3) Or, finally, did the council intend to adhere as closely as possible to the traditional teaching while, at the same time, not try to claim more for that traditional teaching than contemporary scholarship and pastoral experience would allow?

There are three separate hypotheses embodied in these questions. How they are sorted out, one from the other, tells the story of the origins of Theory C.

Hypothesis 1: The council did make some major advances on

the question of co-responsibility in the Church, particularly with its teaching on collegiality in the third chapter of the Dogmatic Constitution on the Church and in its discussion of the laity in the fourth chapter of the same document; but then it hastened to add that none of this material could be regarded as prejudicial to the primacy and jurisdiction of the Pope. The council also expanded our notion of the Body of Christ to include, it would seem, Protestants and other non-Catholic Christians; but the council also continued to insist on the special place of the Catholic Church and on the intrinsic obligation of all mankind to join it. Thus the council consciously neutralized all of its progressive statements.

There is much external evidence to support this first hypothesis. In many places throughout the Catholic world, diocesan pastoral councils and parish councils, to cite but two means of implementing the doctrine of collegiality, do not even exist, and where they exist they are often weak and ineffective. Furthermore, the various directives that have been issued on ecumenism since Vatican II tend to reflect the view that the only really important conciliar texts are those which reaffirm the traditional theology operative before the council. Thus intercommunion occurs only outside the limits of ecclesiastical law and the striking conclusions of the various bilateral conversations which have occurred in the United States since 1965 are generally disregarded.

Hypothesis 2: It is also possible that some of the apparent inconsistency in the documents of Vatican II arose from the complexity of the drafting process. There were sixteen documents. These were developed over a period of four annual sessions by many different committees.

There is some internal evidence to support this second hypothesis. The Dogmatic Constitution on the Church, for example, went through four major drafts. Sometimes changes were made at the last minute (e.g., the addition of the material in Article 5 of that particular constitution) without adequate time or inclination to rewrite other portions of the document which were at least indirectly affected by the new material.

Hypothesis 3: While there is some truth, supported by evidence, in the first two hypotheses, the third view is strongest of all; namely, that the council was keenly aware of theological pluralism and did not wish to close discussion prematurely on any major issue. Condemnation (even of Theory A) was simply not the style of Vatican II. On the other hand, the council was not prepared to endorse officially the various newer views, at least not without some qualification. Thus collegiality could be accepted, but not with prejudice to the papacy. Ecumenism could be approved, but not with prejudice to Catholic distinctiveness. The lay apostolate could be promoted, but not with prejudice to the hierarchical nature of the Church. And so on. If Vatican II is seen as a beginning rather than as an end (Theory B Catholics tend to see it only as an end), these inconsistencies become more apparent than real. The council was not closing discussion so much as opening it.

Few positions (apart from faith in the reality of God, the Lordship of Jesus, or the reconciling power of the Holy Spirit) receive total, unqualified support in the council documents. But there are several other positions which seem to have been accepted in principle, the qualifying phrases notwithstanding. "The seeds are there, like unopened buds awaiting the sun," Cardinal Suenens suggested.[82] "The necessary and salutary reflection of the Church about itself in Vatican II will not be the final stage of theology," Karl Rahner noted. "Another even more important one will come, for which this Council will be seen to have been simply a forerunner and indirect preparation."[83]

Thus, the charismatic movement and related efforts to cultivate the experience of community can be justified as a legitimate extension of the council's teaching that the Church is a community (People of God) before it is a hierarchically structured institution of salvation. Order, in other words, is always at the service of community, and community, in turn, is the product of the supremely unpredictable Spirit.

Second, the growth of organizations such as the National Federation of Priests' Councils, the debate about *Humanae Vitae*, pressure for opening the leadership selection process, and so forth, can be justified as a legitimate extension of the council's teaching on the Church's collegial, nonmonarchical nature.

Pressure for making parish councils deliberative bodies and for the ordination of women reflect that element of the conciliar teaching which underlines the universality of the call to mission and the fundamental equality of all Christians in the fulfillment of that mission.

The changes in clerical self-understanding and the insistence of many priests that they be granted some options in the exercise of their ministry can be viewed as a legitimate application of the conciliar teaching on the universality of the call to holiness; namely, that priests do not constitute an ecclesiastical elite and marriage does not represent some kind of compromise with the gospel.

The new, militant activism of the Berrigans and the political involvement of the Drinans can be perceived as a way of implementing the conciliar teaching that the mission of the Church embraces *diakonia* as constitutively as it embraces preaching and sacramental celebration. Here the conciliar teaching is reinforced by the more recent pronouncement of the Third International Synod of Bishops, "Justice in the World."

The startling advances achieved by the several bilateral ecumenical conversations and the new pressure for intercommunion and the mutual recognition of ministries can be justified on the basis of the conciliar teaching that the Body of Christ embraces more than Roman Catholic Christians. Thus if non-Catholic churches are, to a degree, valid expressions of Christ's Body, then, to that same degree, are their ministries and sacraments valid.

The new emphasis on dialogue even with nonbelievers and

on the importance of freedom even within the Church itself follow from two basic conciliar teachings: (1) that all mankind, explicitly or not, is called to collaborate in the coming of the Kingdom of God; and (2) that no one, even believers, can be compelled to accept a burden which is not absolutely necessary for the purity of faith or the unity of the Church.

Finally, the new wave of criticism, while not uniformly justifiable, can be perceived as utterly scandalous and wholly without merit only by those who continue to identify the Church with the Kingdom of God. The council did distinguish between these two realities, at least inferentially, but it failed to carry through with the important implications of this distinction. For if the Church is not yet the Kingdom, it, too, must come under prophetic judgment.

The method used in each of these cases should be clear. Theory C takes a principle enunciated by the council, disengages it from the residue of Theory A (which accounts for the ambivalence of conciliar teaching), and sets it in a different context, bringing into greater relief the element or elements that are new and distinctive. A more specific application of Theory C will be provided in the next chapter. It is enough to have indicated here that Theory C represents, for the most part, a critical assimilation of Theory B, with an italicizing of those elements in Theory B which reflect a genuine advance beyond Theory A.

The thesis of this chapter has been that the Catholic Church, and parallel religious institutions, have suffered excessive conflict and polarization because its theological self-understanding has not kept pace with the process of institutional change. If the Church's leadership had been able to communicate the theoretical justification for change before, or at least at the same time as, that change occurred, it is likely that the institutional disarray would have been much less severe. But the leadership had already committed two fundamental mistakes in judgment.

First, it thought that it could maintain the unity of the Church more effectively by suppressing free discussion of theological and pastoral issues in the years preceding Vatican II; and, second, once it belatedly recognized the need for some institutional change, the leadership thought that it could introduce that change under entirely controlled circumstances, by imposing the conciliar reforms from above, without adequate preparation of those whom the changes would most immediately affect.

The first error alienated the Church's progressive left and also closed off important channels of popular communication. In other words, had theologians and other scholars in the preconciliar period been given permission to do then what they are doing now anyway, without regard for official ecclesiastical approval, problems would have been identified before, not after, the important decisions had been made. And the second error alienated the Church's conservative-to-traditionalist right by compelling them to act in a spiritually and intellectually schizophrenic manner. The assorted resentments, especially of the extreme right, are entirely understandable and completely predictable.

Yves Congar's assessment of the postconciliar situation is not so dissimilar from mine: ruptures and crises followed Vatican II because "a too long period of narrowness and ossification had stifled initiative: once the valves were opened, the flood was all the heavier because it had the forces of all the currents of the age behind it." Furthermore, "the Vatican II reform was a reform made from above—a fairly unusual phenomenon—which was not prepared from below."[84]

All social conflict is an outgrowth, after all, of conflict in perception. New and different perceptions cannot be imposed from on high. Neither can they have a normal, healthy birth if they have been the victims of several, albeit unsuccessful, abortion attempts. Such perceptions must be freely accepted if they are to become the basis for changes in behavior. If, on the other hand, changes in behavior are legislated and enforced, even before those affected by the behavioral changes have been able to identify and understand the reasons, then such changes can never be more than short-term and temporary. At the first opportunity, people who have been compelled to follow new modes of behavior will revert to those modes to which their abiding perceptions can alone give meaning. That, of course, is exactly what is happening in the Church today. It is a Church in which perception and behavior, theory and practice, do not often correspond one to another.[85] If that situation remains uncorrected, the current process of deterioration will continue.

The proposals offered in the next chapter are designed to challenge and alter that situation. They constitute an agenda for reform, whose immediate goal is the remaking of the Church.

CHAPTER III

An Agenda for Reform

IF THE PRESENT crisis within the Catholic Church is the product of a theory-and-practice gap, as described in the preceding chapter, then one can legitimately conclude that a constructive resolution of the crisis depends in very large measure on the closing of this gap. Practices, both institutional and personal, will have to be brought into conformity with the best theory; and alternate theories will have to be modified to correspond with the practical reality. If such a convergence of theory and practice does not in fact take place, then it is difficult to see how the Church can change its present course toward increasing institutional dissolution. Societies and communities cannot tolerate long-term intellectual and practical schizophrenia, and remain viable and healthy, any more than individuals can.

This view, of course, is shared by many others outside the formal discipline of theology. A canonical colloquium sponsored by the School of Canon Law at the Catholic University of America in May 1972 declared:

> On the one hand, through Vatican II and the theological developments following it, the whole community is gradually appropriating a new vision of the Church and of its life, including priestly life and ministry. On the other hand, the present legal system of the Western Church dates back more than sixty years and originated in a significantly different understanding of the life of the Christian community. This growing discrepancy between vision and law gives rise to increasing tension. It creates a need for greater flexibility and instruments of harmony, since a community cannot long remain strong with a new understanding of its goals and an old set of norms to realize them.[1]

I have been arguing throughout this book that differing attitudes on practical matters are only symptomatic of differing attitudes on theoretical questions. Catholics reject proposals for widening the process for selecting bishops, for example, not because they think the present system produces better leaders, but because they think that no other system can be reconciled with the divine plan. The Church is a monarchical institution by the will of Christ. Who becomes a bishop is a matter of such importance (since it involves adding yet another link in the chain of apostolic succession) that it must be reserved to the Church's absolute monarch, the Pope. Similarly, Catholics reject proposals for expanding the conditions under which Catholics and Protestants can participate in a common Eucharist, not because they dislike Protestants or regard them as inferior people, but because they perceive intercommunion of any kind, under any circumstances, as a compromise of the fundamental principle that the Catholic Church is the "one, true Church of Christ" and that all other Christian communities can be nothing more than ecclesiastical pretenders, without valid ministries or sacraments. Finally, Catholics reject the idea of deliberative parish councils (and their equivalents at other levels of ecclesiastical life), not because they distrust the judgment of nonordained Christians or because they entertain the naïve notion that priests are invested with the fullness of wisdom and sound judgment, but because they perceive the Church as a hierarchically structured, visible society, founded and organized from the top down, according to a pyramid model. Decision-making must be unilateral; the Church, after all, is not a democracy. And so the process goes.

The judgment set forth in the preceding paragraph is empirically substantiated, in part at least, by the recent sociological investigation of the American Catholic priesthood, conducted by the National Opinion Research Center, University of Chicago, under the direction of the Reverend Andrew M. Greeley. In one of the most striking conclusions of the report, the authors cite the following as the first of eight "serious problems" facing the priesthood:

> Large numbers of priests are dissatisfied with the way the ecclesiastical structure is shaped and the way decision-making power is distributed; but the leadership of the Church does not share this dissatisfaction. Furthermore, it would appear that differences between younger and older priests on the distribution of power and authority are rooted in ideological differences about the nature of the Church and religion.[2]

I shall offer in this chapter some specific proposals which, in my judgment and in the judgment of various formal groups and professional societies in the contemporary Catholic Church, belong on any agenda of serious ecclesiastical reform. In each instance, I shall identify the ecclesiological assumptions which inform the usual objections to these proposals, and I shall also recall and underline the relevant theological principles which can legitimate these reform measures. There are thirteen proposals in all. They are reducible to two principal goals: (1) to bring the organizational operations of the Church into conformity with, and place them at the service of, the historic goals, or mission, of that Church; and (2) to draw upon the resources of the whole Church in the fulfillment of this mission, by motivating the general membership to accept and pursue the Church's goals. This can happen only if the membership is allowed and encouraged to participate actively in the various processes through which these goals are identified and achieved. Our abiding concern, therefore, is with the quality and exercise of leadership. It is the leadership of an organization which clarifies organizational goals and which motivates people to accept and pursue those goals. The leadership also exercises major control over the institutional processes by which these goals are pursued. In the absence of a coup d'état of one kind or another, institutional change comes only after those in positions of official leadership are persuaded, gradually or suddenly by force of events outside their immediate control, to channel their power toward institutional transformation. Furthermore, the rank-and-file of any organization—and the Church is no exception—will not apply themselves to the pursuit of that organization's goals if they do not perceive those goals as inseparable from their own personal goals. The task of demonstrating the connection between organizational objectives and personal objectives is a function of leadership. Leadership, in other words, is responsible for identifying and clarifying goals, on the one hand, and for motivating people to accept and pursue those goals, on the other hand.

The Problem of Institutional Response

There is no such thing as a perfect organization or a perfect society, certain claims to that effect notwithstanding. But the theoretical plan of such an ideal organization serves a useful purpose in helping us to evaluate the nature, and to study the direction, of actual organizations. We can measure organizational responses against hypothetical norms of perfection.

An inevitable organizational pathology is its tendency to maintain institutional equilibrium. Organizations, even radical, left-wing, revolutionary societies, are institutionally conservative. It is the rare organization indeed that votes itself out of existence once it recognizes that its original purposes have already been fulfilled.

However, the environment in which an organization finds itself will not permit it to remain at rest. The environment constantly stimulates the organization and impinges upon it, ultimately forcing it, over the long run, and sometimes even suddenly over the short run, to make changes or perish. It is this interaction between the conservative tendency toward equilibrium (maintaining the status quo), on the one hand, and the external disturbances, on the other hand, which causes various changes in the organization. The organization's response to this tension can go in four directions, one of which we can set aside at once; namely, its complete destruction. The other three directions have been designated in different ways, e.g., the way of tenacity, the way of elasticity, and the way of self-determination. How the organization responds to its environment and to the pressure for change depends on its particular structure.[3]

The three options can be illustrated by the elements in the following example: a rock (the way of tenacity), some kelp (the way of elasticity), and a porpoise (the way of self-determination), with the ocean serving as the common environment (see Glossary, p. 168). The rock neither gives nor interacts with the ocean any more than can be helped. Water wears it away and it does nothing to rebuild itself, relying instead on its integrality to continue its existence. The kelp, on the other hand, has some of the resistant features of the rock and is also, to some extent at least, self-determinative, but generally it relies on its elasticity to preserve its integrality. It allows itself to give and to yield to the conformations imposed upon it by the tides, the currents, etc., but it still manages to interact with the ocean in such a manner as to preserve itself. Finally, there is the porpoise which, unlike the rock and the kelp, can control to a great degree its interactions with its watery environment. It can go after food or not; it can swim against the tide and current; its time and energy are not totally taken up with maintaining itself in existence.

The ways of tenacity and elasticity seem to be at least as good as that of self-determination, if mere survival alone is at issue. Indeed, they may even be better. But in terms of the perfect organization, they have settled the problem of integrality at too low a level. They have compromised too soon, having closed off any chance of real growth toward perfection. Self-determination, on the other hand, is a way which alone offers the possibility of continual improvement, and self-determination alone gives the opportunity for working toward the ideal. However, there is a price to be paid. The organization must be prepared to sacrifice a large amount of its integrality, i.e., it cannot act as if it were a completely closed, totally self-sufficient system *(societas perfecta!)*. It must continually invest itself, taking the essential risks inherent in the investment process. The organization cannot stand pat.

While the Church is a mystery, it is also a human institution. Monophysitism is no less heretical for ecclesiology than it is for Christology. As a human institution, it follows, to a greater or lesser degree, the laws of organizational behavior. As a mystery, i.e., as the sacrament of Christ and of God, it is forever called to perfection. Organizational theory, however, insists that the perfect organization neither exists nor can exist in this world order. Such theory is validated by theology, and specifically by eschatology. On this side of the Parousia nothing can be identified completely with the Kingdom of God. Everything, including the Church, labors under some measure of imperfection. The Church is always on the way, but not yet there. In the meantime, everything is to be judged by the final goal. All reality is subordinated to, and measured against, the promised future, the fully realized Kingdom. Just as it is proper to hold aloft the Kingdom of God as the transcendent goal and norm of our present moral strivings, so it is proper to hold aloft the ideal of the perfect organization as the ultimate goal and norm of our present institutional strivings.

Every organization's fundamental tendency is toward self-preservation. If institutions could remain completely at rest, they would do so, but then, of course, they would die. That which does not change at all is dead. Every organization, however, finds itself in a given environment which will not allow the organization to remain at rest. The environment constantly stimulates and impinges upon the organization, forcing it to change or to perish. There is in every organization, including the Church as well, a tension created by this dialectical interaction between the organization's conservative tendency to maintain equilibrium and the various external disturbances ("signs of the times"?).

The Church's institutional response can follow four paths. The first we rule out; namely, the way of complete destruction. Adopting that response, the Church would sadly decide that the interaction is not worth the energy and so would simply stop functioning: a kind of self-administered euthanasia. This may be a response of sorts, but it is one that is hardly viable. Indeed, there would be no point at all to this book if I were to judge it so.

This leaves the Church with three other choices. Each of these choices, I should strenuously argue, is based upon three separate theologies of the Church. Theory and practice are inextricably linked. The first choice—the way of tenacity—is based on the assumption that the Church is so thoroughly divine in nature that its human character is really insignificant. The human side of the Church is but the mindlessly pliant instrument of the divine, a relationship conceived in much the same way as some nineteenth-century Catholic theologians assumed that the human writer of Sacred Scripture functioned at a level no more self-determinative than that of a guitar pick in a musician's fingers.[4] Thus, since the Church is, for all practical purposes, totally divine, it cannot endure or tolerate substantial institutional change. The institutions, after all, are the external expression of the divine presence. To tamper with ecclesiastical structures is to tamper with the reality of God. Accordingly, the Church may be in the world, but it is surely not of the world. The world is somehow separate from the Church. The Church is over against the world, existing there as a ghetto in a city, or a diplomatic sanctuary in a battle zone, or a cyst in an organism: taking what it can, but giving nothing in return. To give in return would constitute interaction, and interaction would end its status as a wholly separate, totally self-contained organization.

But like the rock, this kind of Church cannot completely avoid the effects of its environment. Something of its institutional self is bound to be worn away gradually, as we see it happening today, although not so gradually. And yet, by the force of its own rigid theology, that Church can do nothing to rebuild itself. The Lord may give, and the Lord may take away, but man can do nothing. The Theory A Catholic, who prefers the way of tenacity as a matter of theological principle, perceives as well as anyone else the attrition process now at work in the Church. He has an explanation, and he has a response. The explanation is that God is testing his people, summoning them to heroic steadfastness and fidelity in a time of material reversal; the response is to hold the line, to stand firm, and to do whatever one can to restore the institutional elements of the status quo ante. Such a Church, of course, is no longer on the road to perfection. Improvement is rendered impossible. Furthermore, this view of the Church cannot be reconciled with the Church's own official self-understanding. The Theory A Catholic, who proudly asserts his loyalty to church doctrine, finds himself strangely and uncomfortably out of step with some significant elements of that doctrine. The Church is not over against the world; it is *in* the world. Indeed, the Church is that part of the world which alone confesses and celebrates the Lordship of Jesus Christ. But its mission is to the world, for the sake of the Kingdom. The Church must discern the redemptive presence of God and respond creatively and courageously to that presence, facilitating the divine entrance, enabling it to break through and renew the face of the earth.[5] The Catholic Church has officially eschewed the way of tenacity. It has chosen some other institutional response. It has done so because —the truth must be stated bluntly and boldly—the Catholic Church no longer accepts Theory A as an expression of its official self-understanding.

The second choice—the way of elasticity—is based on the assumption that the Church is so human and so relative an organization that its abiding, spiritual elements are really insignificant. The Church must be, first and foremost, a spearhead for social reform or a locus for interpersonal encounter.

Whether it preserves the historic Eucharist, whether it remains faithful to the doctrinal tradition of earlier ecumenical councils, whether it retains an ordained ministry—these concerns are entirely secondary. If, on the one hand, the Church is where the action is, or, on the other hand, the Church makes personal growth possible, then nothing else is finally important. In a time of change, the Church's only reasonable response can be to move with the times, to test the waters, to put its ear to the ground. Any structures will do, so long as these purposes are promoted.

But like the kelp, this kind of Church can interact with its environment only to the point where it can preserve itself in existence. If it loses its "relevance," it is dead. It is a Church, therefore, ever in pursuit of the new, the popular, the trendy —and ever at their mercy. The terms are set exclusively by the environment. The Church, in this view, is an organization without initiative, without anything distinctive to contribute, without any special resources of its own. To the Theory A Catholic, all institutional reform is an expression of mindless elasticity. He is right in challenging the way of elasticity as a viable means of achieving ecclesiastical renewal, but he is wrong in concluding that every effort toward institutional reform is an exercise in compromise and retreat. The way of elasticity, to be sure, is wrong because it devaluates those elements of the Church which make the Christian community historically distinctive. The Church is set apart from all other communities, societies, and institutions by reason of its corporate conviction, rooted in its New Testament origins, that Jesus of Nazareth is "the key, the focal point, and the goal of all human history."[6] Jesus alone is the Lord and Christ of history. The company of his disciples must be obedient to the Lord's will by breaking the bread of his body and sharing the cup of his blood, until he comes (Acts 2:42). It is a community called upon to embody his presence beyond his own time, and to make straight the paths to the Kingdom of God at the end. Its mission must indeed include social action *(diakonia)* and the Church must be for its members and all others a place where human growth occurs through the experience of community *(koinonia)*. But it remains nonetheless the one community wherein the Lordship of Jesus and the power of his Spirit is proclaimed and celebrated, or else it is not longer the Church at all.[7]

The ways of tenacity and elasticity can ensure a temporary, even long-term, survival of sorts, but the Church is called to a higher purpose than mere institutional survival. It is a living organism, the Body of Christ, a Spirit-filled community. Where the Spirit is, there must be life. If it is Christ's Body, then it must be a living body. The Risen Lord lives! A ghetto Church, holding the line against the winds of change, but losing the war inch by inch, bears no resemblance to the eschatological community of the New Testament, utterly committed to the coming reign of God, a community open to the future, a Church of supreme hope. Neither does a flaccid Church, with a wet thumb in every breeze, and losing its soul in the process, bear any resemblance to the tiny company of disciples who embraced the crown of martyrdom rather than deny their Lord and God. The Church of the New Testament was a community holding fast to the teachings it had been given, faithfully celebrating the Lord's Supper until the day of final redemption.[8]

The third choice, the way of self-determination, is based on the assumption that the Church is a mystery: a visible, human sign of the invisible presence of the transcendent God in the midst of the world. The Church's own transcendent character forecloses the way of elasticity; its fully human, institutional character forecloses the way of tenacity. The way of self-determination alone offers the possibility of continual improvement. The door to perfection is not prematurely shut. The ideal remains the norm and the goal. But there is a price to be paid. The Church must give as well as take, let go as well as hold fast. It must continually invest its resources and accept the risks that accompany such investment.

Like the porpoise, the Church controls to a great degree its interactions with the changing environment. Such a Church can still take initiatives. No longer preoccupied with survival, while living along the margin of social existence, the Church can move here and there as it discerns the presence of the Spirit of God. If God is not bound to sacred precincts, neither can that community be bound which calls itself his People.[9]

The Problem of Motivation

Institutional reform is impossible unless the people whom the institution embraces become willing, and indeed enthusiastic, participants in the process of reform. This raises the question of motivation.

In any organization there are differences in performance among people doing the same kind of work. These differences reflect not only differences in ability but also differences in motivation. At any given point in time people vary in the extent to which they are willing to direct their energies toward the attainment of an organization's objectives.

The problem of motivating employees in a business or in any corporate enterprise is as old as organized activity itself, but it is only within the last fifty years that the scientific method has been brought to bear on its solution. There are at least three major approaches to the problem of personal motivation within organizations: the way of paternalism, the way of scientific management, and the way of participative management (see Glossary, p. 168).[10]

The paternalistic method assumes that people who are satisfied with their job will more likely be effective at that job. The more one rewards the worker, the harder he works. His motivation is essentially one of gratitude and loyalty. The essence of this approach is to make an organization a source of important rewards—rewards for which the only qualification is membership in the organization (e.g., pension plans, group insurance, subsidized education, recreation programs, comfortable working conditions, across-the-board wage increases, job security, and predictable promotion patterns).

But there is little evidence that any of these policies has had a direct effect on worker productivity or performance. The relevant distinction here is between a person's satisfaction with the job and his motivation to perform effectively in that job. It was once assumed, incorrectly, that these two things went hand in hand, that a person who was satisfied with his job would necessarily be effective at it. During the last twenty years or so there have been large numbers of research studies conducted to test the accuracy of this assumption, and these studies have shown no consistent or meaningful relationship between job satisfaction and effective performance. Effective performers were as likely to be dissatisfied with their jobs as they were to be satisfied, and vice versa.[11] It might be concluded, therefore, that the paternalistic approach has not been a very effective strategy for resolving the problem of motivation.

The scientific management method assumes, on the other hand, that a person will be motivated to work if rewards and penalties are attached directly to his performance. Thus, rewards are conditional, not unconditional. They are contingent upon effective performance (e.g., wage incentives, promotion on the basis of merit, recognizing and rewarding special accomplishment). Penalties are meted out for failure (e.g., warnings, reprimands, even dismissals). This second method depends on an external control system and is based on the principle of reinforcement, i.e., if a person undertakes an action and this action is followed by a reward, the probability that the action will be repeated is increased, and vice versa.

This method, too, has severe limitations. There are an exceedingly large number of outcomes which are potentially gratifying or aversive to human beings and only a small number of these outcomes are under direct managerial control. It is particularly difficult for the external control system to encompass the higher order of needs for esteem and self-actualization, as detailed by Abraham Maslow.[12] Indeed, certain rewards and penalties relevant to social needs are under the control of the informal organization, and these sanctions may work against the formal control system. A second limitation to the external control system is its reliance on some reasonably objective method of measuring or assessing performance. As the organization's complexity increases, the variables increase with it. Meanwhile, the possibility of total control decreases proportionately.

The participative management method assumes that individuals can derive satisfaction from doing an effective job per se. They can become personally involved in their work, taking pride in the evidence that they are effectively promoting the objectives of the organization. One of the basic elements of the different theories of participative management is the integration of the planning and the doing. The person is given broad goals or objectives and is enabled and encouraged to determine for himself how they are to be achieved. This makes the job more of a challenge than if the person were simply told what to do and when to do it. A second common element in these theories is the reduction in the use of authority as a means of control. The supervisor or manager plays a helping role rather than an authoritative one. Finally, there is much more reliance on the use of work groups as problem-solving and decision-making units. Where decisions affect a whole unit, the supervisor meets with all those affected by the potential decision and encourages them to participate in the process of finding a solution. The opportunity to participate in the decision-making process creates a sense of involvement and commitment on the part of the affected individuals and enhances identification of their personal goals with the corporate goals and objectives of the organization.[13]

The applicability of the preceding discussion to the problem of ecclesiastical reform should be clear. Those who perceive the

Church according to Theory A will generally opt for the paternalistic method of organizational management. Membership in the Church automatically confers benefits available to all on an equal basis. One is already within the Kingdom of God. All are given the gifts of faith, hope, and charity. All have the right to receive the sacraments. And when we move from the general to the particular (e.g., to the ordained ministry of the Church), the paternalistic method is even more apparent. Priests are related to their bishop as sons to father. By the very fact of ordination the priest is guaranteed a lifetime occupation, with group insurance, retirement plans, subsidized education, comfortable working conditions, wage increases based on years of ordination, job security, and predictable promotion patterns based on seniority. But there is no evidence that materially comfortable working conditions make priests more effective or give them a greater sense of identification with the mission of the whole Church. On the contrary, large numbers of priests are dissatisfied with the way the ecclesiastical structure is shaped and the way decision-making power is distributed. Significantly, the leadership does not share this dissatisfaction.[14]

The scientific management method is perhaps lodged somewhere between Theory A and Theory B. It retains some of the values of Theory A insofar as it employs an external control system; and it moves closer to Theory B insofar as it cherishes competence and has high regard for professional standards. But there is a limit to what professionalization can accomplish. Catholics, and priests in particular (to continue with our earlier example), need more than hierarchical approval or the incentive of recognition and promotion based on merit. They have certain needs which the organization alone cannot fulfill.

Those who understand the Church as the whole People of God, wherein all—laity, religious, and clergy alike—are responsible for the mission of the Church, are drawn to the participative management approach. The most important question for the Church is not how it is to be governed or how it is to be structured, but what it is to do. The membership of the Church must know, first of all, what their purpose is, what their goals are; and then they must be encouraged and motivated to pursue those goals, not as something extrinsic to themselves but as something identifiable with their own personal goals. Since all are responsible for the mission in the first instance, all must be involved somehow in the process by which that responsibility is determined and exercised.

Furthermore, the Theory C Catholic understands that the Church is a collegial, not a monarchical, organization. Authority is not dominative, but diaconal. The bishop and pastor stand in the midst of the community as those who serve. Problems that affect a particular group must be solved, whenever possible, at the level of that particular group. In the Catholic social encyclicals this was known as the principle of subsidiarity. The opportunity to participate in the decision-making process creates a sense of involvement and commitment on the part of the affected church members and helps them to perceive, if such is indeed the case, that the corporate goals of the Church are not at cross-purposes with their own goals; on the contrary, that the Church's goals and their own are fundamentally the same. To further the mission of the Church is to further the good of oneself and of one's loved ones.

Maslow has suggested that the principles of participative management are most useful in managing persons with strong needs for self-actualization.[15] The Christian is called to put on Christ, to grow up in him, to become a new creature (2 Cor. 5:17)—it is a rhetoric not of stagnation but of growth, development, and actualization. Just as the ways of tenacity and elasticity work against the possibility of the Church's growth toward perfection, so the ways of paternalism and scientific management (reinforcement) work against the possibility of the individual Christian's growth toward perfection. The two areas, of institutional response and of motivation, thereby converge. Institutional reform requires the way of self-determination;

motivation for mission requires the way of participative management. Autocratic leadership and unilateral decision-making, although sanctioned by Theory A, will inevitably frustrate—and have frustrated—the very purpose for which such leadership is consciously exercised: the Church's growth in holiness, its advance toward perfection, its movement toward the final Kingdom of God. In the final analysis, we find that good organizational and motivational theory corresponds with good canonical and theological principles.

NEXUS

The remainder of this chapter is an exercise in practical ecclesiology. It is an attempt to apply a contemporary theology of the Church (Theory C) in institutional, structural ways; first, by identifying the ineffective and sometimes harmful structures; second, by proposing constructive alternatives; and, third, by identifying the relevant theological principles which are at issue in the debate, both pro and con.

An Agenda for Reform—Problems and Proposals

1. PRINCIPLES OF CONSTITUTIONALISM

The present ecclesiastical system reflects only one phase in the total institutional history of the Church; namely, its feudalistic and monarchical experience. The system does not reflect at all the alternate experience of constitutionalism which the Church itself was, in large part, responsible for initiating in the Western world.[16] The present system exemplifies numerous qualities of monarchical absolutism: Pope and bishops remain for all practical purposes the exclusive rulers in the Church, combining the legislative, executive, and judicial powers in one hand. Despite the recent creation of councils, authority is still exercised in many places without being subject to effective accountability.

Accordingly, the Church must move from a system of monarchical absolutism to some form of constitutionalism which, Brian Tierney has reminded us, "is not something foreign to the tradition of the Catholic Church. If we chose to adopt constitutional forms in the structure of the modern church, we should not be borrowing from an alien system. Rather we should be reclaiming a rich part of our own inheritance."[17]

Constitutionalism involves three basic elements: the limitation of power, accountability, and openness to correction. The limitation of power is achieved by *(a)* a division of power between central and regional governing bodies; *(b)* the separation of legislative, executive, and judicial power; and *(c)* guarantee of individual rights, including due process of law. Accountability is ensured by *(a)* the electoral process; *(b)* freedom of information, whereby the exercise of official power is a matter of public record; and *(c)* freedom of discussion and debate regarding the policy and performance of office holders as well as the ultimate assumptions of the community itself. And, finally, openness to correction is ensured by *(a)* regular meetings of legislative bodies; *(b)* reinterpretation of law by tribunals; and *(c)* permanent commissions charged with the responsibility of proposing legal reforms.[18]

2. DECENTRALIZATION OF POWER

Because power remains concentrated at the top and decisions are formulated there in secret, the rank-and-file among the laity, religious, and clergy have become largely indifferent to the operations of the Church (except in those relatively few instances where the membership have become angry and hostile). The principle of participative management is inoperative. When the decisions of the monarchical leadership are not received with evident enthusiasm, indeed when these decisions are frequently ignored, the officeholder appeals to his divinely given authority and reminds the membership of their duty to obey it. But the motivation remains extrinsic: accept what has been decreed (even in the case of Vatican II directives), not because of its intrinsic merit, but because it bears the stamp of official approval.

Accordingly, the Church must put into practice at once its own time-honored principle of subsidiarity that a higher agency or group should never do for a lower agency or group what that lower agency or group can do for itself. There must be a decentralization of power which restores to particular churches their ancient freedom to adapt the discipline of the Christian life and ministry to their own distinctive needs and situation.[19] Parish councils, diocesan pastoral councils, and national pastoral councils must become more than rubber-stamp agencies. (The denial of a local church's right to establish such councils is theologically and pastorally outrageous. And yet, for all practical purposes, that is what the Vatican did when, in early 1973, it forbade the Church in Holland to convene its national pastoral council.) Such councils must have deliberative as well as consultative power. They should be, in other words, the policy-making bodies for their own communities. At all levels these fundamental conditions must be fulfilled: *(a)* the body should meet regularly according to its own rules; *(b)* the body should choose its own officers and determine its own rules of procedure and agenda; *(c)* the deliberations of the body should be open and should be publicized; *(d)* the body should have its own secretariat, with full access to relevant information and with the assistance of experts.[20]

3. Planning and Research

The Catholic Church has at present no institution dedicated to research and planning. There is perhaps no other large organization in the modern world which has less idea of what it is doing, how much it is accomplishing, or where it is going, than does the Catholic Church. Social research is identified with the gathering of statistics to provide *ad hoc* answers to specific questions. Information-gathering proceeds according to uneven and often unreliable methods, and policy planning, which comparable organizations regard as absolutely essential, has hardly existed at all. Of course, if one insists that the Church's response to its environment must be the way of tenacity, then the need for research and planning is minimal or nonexistent. If, on the other hand, one regards the path of self-determination as the only theologically and pastorally viable response on the part of the ecclesiastical institution, then planning and research become as essential to the Church as they clearly are to any similarly complex organization.

Accordingly, *(a)* offices devoted to research and planning for the long-range development of the Church are necessary at the central, national, diocesan, and parish levels; so, too, *(b)* an office of financial management; *(c)* permanent means of assessing public opinion in the Church; and *(d)* a public relations department whose function would be to provide information to church members and the public at large on policies, procedures, and related matters.[21]

4. PRINCIPLES OF ACCOUNTABILITY

Neither does the Church have any agency committed to supervising the collective operations of the whole ecclesiastical machinery. Decisions affecting large numbers of people and large amounts of money are made day after day, at international, national, and diocesan levels. These really important decisions are made in secret, but even after they have become public, the rank-and-file membership of the Church have no institutionalized recourse against those decisions. They are forced to use the power of publicity in the hopes of embarrassing the leadership and forcing it to reconsider its initial judgment.

Accordingly, the Church needs a public adversary system which will provide a check and balance in this area. The explicit responsibility of such a system would be the development and presentation of an effective adversary position on each project or activity funded by the leadership, to assess them for fidelity to the interests of the whole Church and to its mission. The duties of the adversary agency would include effective investigation into sloppy management procedures, hidden expenditures, and performance. The adversary system would also be charged with questioning the need for every program, developing alternate ideas and approaches, and establishing machinery for the constructive, ongoing evaluation of the pros and cons of each issue. To avoid the development of its own internal bureaucracy and the establishment of an unhealthy symbiotic relationship between itself and its assigned agency or agencies within the Church, each adversary project should be terminated and its functions wholly abolished after a period of three years. A different project team and apparatus would then be formed to assess and criticize the project for the next three-year period. Funding for this adversary system could be based on this formula: 1 percent of the total amount appropriated for any given project would finance the adversary process.[22]

5. SELECTION OF BISHOPS

Bishops are still chosen in the Catholic Church according to the criterion of conformity. Any one of the hundreds of Catholic pastors, teachers, educators, administrators, theologians, catechists, journalists, sociologists, psychologists, and so forth, who associated himself with the public dissent against *Humanae Vitae* is automatically disqualified, under present standards, for advancement to this office of pastoral leadership. And yet 70 percent of the American Catholic priests surveyed in the National Opinion Research Center (NORC) study supported the election of bishops by the clergy of the diocese,[23] a position which is entirely in accord not only with the ancient canonical principle that "he who governs all should be elected by all," but also with the ancient and long-standing practice of the election of bishops by the clergy and laity.[24]

Accordingly, the Church must return at once to its adherence to both the principle and the practice. It is essential that the process include all the major elements within a given local community, selected by the diocesan pastoral council from its own members: diocesan priests, religious men and women, laywomen and laymen. The committee for the selection of bishops should have a limited term of office, although for the sake of continuity the terms of the individual members ought not to terminate all at the same time. It is also essential that this selection committee be fully informed of the needs of the diocese and have access to every kind of information it may require to make responsible judgments about the various candidates. It is equally imperative that the committee consult as widely as possible and encourage public discussion. Existing recommendations for reform in this area are inadequate because they leave unchallenged the power of outside bishops, papal delegates, and the Pope himself in the final selection process.[25] A bishop should be the choice principally of the community he is to serve. An agreed-upon nominee who meets opposition from external sources should not thereby be rejected, except after public discussion involving the full disclosure of reasons for such opposition. In the end, the Pope accepts rather than approves the decision of the local church.

If one grants a central argument of this book, that the present crisis in the Catholic Church involves a crisis of confidence in its leadership, then this kind of change has more immediate pastoral import than most of the other recommendations included herein.

6. PAPAL POWER

One of the major elements in the Theory A ecclesiology was its italicization of the papacy in the life and mission of the Church.

Even the cautious scholar Yves Congar has acknowledged that the power and importance of the Pope have been exaggerated since the First Vatican Council and particularly during the pontificate of Pius XII.[26] Many Catholics still have the idea that all of the Pope's judgments, at whatever level they are expressed (encyclicals, decrees, sermons, comments to pilgrims, reported comments in L'Osservatore Romano, etc.), are to be accepted as true. For all practical purposes, the Pope is never wrong; to criticize him, however, is always wrong. There has been such an identification of the Pope with Christ (Vicarius Christi) that one is led even to the conclusion that to differ with the Pope is to differ with the Lord himself. Canonically, of course, the authority of the Pope is supreme and unchallengeable. His decisions are final, and no other major decisions are final until they have received his approval: whether the issue is priestly celibacy, the appointment of bishops, the admission of women to the priesthood, or the substitution of vegetable oil for olive oil in the administration of the sacrament of the sick.

Accordingly, the Church must willingly, and perhaps painfully, demythologize its understanding of the papacy, bringing its perceptions into greater conformity with New Testament and historical scholarship and contemporary theological reflection.[27] While he remains the symbol of faith and unity for all the churches of the world, and while his office retains, in principle, the greatest authority for moral and doctrinal utterance, the Pope himself can no longer function as an absolute monarch, embodying in his single person all executive, legislative, and judicial power—without limitation, without accountability, without the possibility of correction.

General policy decisions affecting the universal Church should be reserved, not to the Pope alone, but to the Pope and the International Synod of Bishops. The function of the Curia is to assist in the execution of these decisions. In the course of such execution, the Curia may issue administrative directives concerned with interdiocesan or supranational questions, but it should have no administrative authority in purely local matters.

Problems which are national, not international, in character should be within the competence of the national conference of bishops rather than the Pope, and the same would be true of problems at regional and diocesan levels, in keeping with the Church's fundamental principle of subsidiarity. The election of the Pope by the International Synod of Bishops rather than by the College of Cardinals and some limitation of tenure (e.g., ten years, renewable) would serve to modify the present absolutely monarchical pattern.[28]

7. EPISCOPAL POWER

What has been said of the papal office is true, in a slightly different sense, of the episcopal office. Many bishops continue to perceive themselves as responsible directly to the Pope alone, as if they were his delegates or vicars within a given administrative subdivision of the one Church. They do not think of the people within their diocese as the constituency to whom they are constantly responsible and accountable. They exercise their authority, not according to the method of participative management, but according to the method of paternalism. And they wonder why their priests, religious, and laity are not universally motivated to collaborate with them in the pursuit of the Church's mission.

Accordingly, the Church must also willingly demythologize its understanding of the episcopal office, bringing its perceptions into greater conformity with New Testament and historical scholarship and contemporary theological reflections.[29] While the bishop shall remain the symbol of faith and unity within the local church, and while his office retains, in principle, great authority for moral and doctrinal utterance, the bishop personally can no longer function within his diocese as its absolute monarch, embodying in himself all executive, legislative, and judicial power, limited only by his personal and canonical loyalties to the Pope.

The diocesan community is to be governed by its pastoral

council, and decisions should be reached on the basis of a consensus of the bishop and the council. The bishop, too, should be selected by the people he is to serve and for a term of office that is limited. Furthermore, the still current practice of a bishop's moving from one diocese to another, as if up a career ladder, should be ended immediately. Finally, the bishop should perceive himself and his diocese as part of a community of bishops and dioceses. By episcopal ordination he is a member of the whole episcopal college, and of its various national and regional segments. He cannot forbid in his community what is legitimately permitted in others. He cannot demand of his people, and especially of his priests and religious, what is not demanded of others in similar circumstances. The highly inequitable treatment of dissenters against *Humanae Vitae* from diocese to diocese is an example of this pastoral discrepancy. Finally, he—and his brother bishops—must recognize that there are other successions besides the succession of their own pastoral office; namely, the successions of prophets and of teachers.[30] Bishops must simply stop identifying the teaching charism with their own offices, as if it did not belong also to the whole Church and particularly to that group in the Church who were known, from New Testament times, as the *didaskaloi* (today's translation: "theologians").[31] If the Church is to be truly reformed, its prophets and theologians will have to assert their independence, not from the Church in whose service they always remain, but from the bishops who are perennially tempted to co-opt and/or control them. The question usually asked after a brief dissertation on the need for complete theological freedom is: "Who, then, will control the theologians?" That question is as theologically intelligible as the questions: "Who, then, will control the bishops?" and "Who will control the Pope?" It is the Spirit alone who guarantees the unity of the Church.[32]

8. A BILL OF RIGHTS

Legal reforms begin with protests within a society against the established government. The protests are specific and concrete; they are centered on individuals and on the punishments imposed on them. The protests engender discussions and debates that soon rise to the level of general principles. There have been many controversies in recent years over violations of the rights of individuals, groups, and institutions. The inadequacy of existing procedures for dealing with such controversies was dramatically illustrated, again, by the events following the publication of *Humanae Vitae*. Many Catholic laity, religious, and clergy are still vulnerable to arbitrary administrative action against their own interests. Where they are spared such unpleasantness, it is more a matter of benign paternalism rather than of legal protection. In the meantime, freedom is demanded for the Church outside, but it is not always granted inside.

Accordingly, a bill of rights ought to be formulated and promulgated throughout the Church, in accordance with an open, collegial process already suggested above, specifying those areas where the protection of Christian freedom is of absolute necessity:

• The right to freedom in the search for truth, without fear of administrative sanctions.

• The right to freedom in expressing personal beliefs and opinions as they appear to the individual, including freedom of communication and publication.

• The right of individuals to access to objective information, in particular about the internal and external operations of the Church (information such as an adversary agency might require).

• The right to develop the unique potentialities and personality traits proper to the individual without fear of repression by the Christian community or church authorities.

• The right of the Christian to work out his salvation in response to the unique challenges offered by the age and society in which he lives.

• The rights of persons employed by, or engaged in the service of, the Church to conditions of work consonant with human dignity as well as the right to professional practices comparable to those in the society at large.

• The right to freedom of assembly and of association (such as the formation of an association of priests, even alongside the established senate of priests in a given diocese).

• The right to participate according to our gifts from the Spirit, in the teaching, government, and sanctification of the Church.

• All the rights and freedoms of Christians without discrimination on the basis of race, color, sex, birth, language, political opinion, or national or social origin.

• The right to effective remedies for the redress of grievances and the vindication of their rights.

• In all proceedings in which one of the parties may suffer substantial disadvantage, the procedure must be fair and impartial, with an opportunity for submission to boards of mediation and arbitration. (Due process has already been accepted in principle by the American Catholic bishops, but it has not yet been adopted in most of the dioceses.)

• In all procedures, administrative or judicial, in which penalties may be imposed, the accused shall not be deprived of any right, office, or communion with the Church except by due process of law; said due process shall include, but not be limited to, the right not to be a witness against oneself; the right to a speedy and public trial; the right to be informed in advance of the specific charge against him; the right to confront the witnesses against him; the right to have the assistance of experts and of counsel for his defense; and a right of appeal.[33]

9. Ecclesiastical Courts

The numbers and spiritual situation of Catholics who remarry after divorce have created a grave pastoral issue within the Church in the United States, and this situation has been seriously aggravated by procedural jurisprudence and personal weaknesses which leave many cases unsolved or insoluble in the external forum. In the meantime, longstanding efforts to resolve such cases in the internal forum have been suspended summarily by a private communication from the Vatican. Most Catholics ignore their Church's marriage tribunals when they find themselves outside the canonical limits by reason of divorce and remarriage.[34] Either they accept their outlaw status and remain away from the sacraments (and perhaps from church entirely) or they decide in the privacy of their own consciences that they are innocent before God and therefore still eligible to receive the sacraments. But there is a tiny minority who do indeed take the Catholic Church's intricate matrimonial procedures to heart. They bring their cases before the Church's courts, expecting a swift and fair hearing. In too many instances, however, their cases have been shunted aside for two and three years, long beyond the time when a decision might retain meaning and purpose. Often they are faced with judges who represent the most extreme right-of-center views on the ecclesiastical spectrum: men of inflexible, rigid, authoritarian, Theory A views.

Accordingly, some substantial revision of the Church's official matrimonial procedures and of its court system is mandatory. Regional courts should be developed under the aegis of the episcopal conferences. Parties should be fully apprised during the proceedings of the evidence upon which the decisions of formal courts will be based, and the parties should be given full opportunity to argue all the issues in dispute. The procedure of these courts should aim at simplicity and speed, for justice delayed is justice denied. Courts should always give reasons for their decisions and should afford opportunity for the expression of judicial dissents. The only criterion for personnel in the courts should be professional competence. No one should be disqualified on grounds of sex or lack of clerical status. Insofar as possible, formal courts should be staffed by fulltime and professionally trained personnel. Judges should be appointed for a term of years. In the interest of their independence, they should not be removable by executive order. The binding interpretation of the laws of the Church, including those pertaining to marriage, should be reserved to the courts; executive offices or commissions should not have the right to make such interpretations. The procedure in marriage cases should be as simple, flexible, and expeditious as possible because: (a) the subject matter of the case is theological, i.e., the existence of a sacrament; (b) the most intimate rights of the parties are concerned; (c) the proceeding is not truly adversary; (d) the relevant evidence can often be collected from the parties themselves; and (e) delay can cause irreparable injustice to the parties and to their children.[35]

Internal forum solutions (as, for example, the allowing of divorced-and-remarried Catholics to receive the sacraments), reached in accordance with sound principles of moral theology, should be respected and not be distorted by excessive administrative regulations such as questionnaires, processes, decrees, records, etc. Episcopal guidelines should take into account the need for instruction of the Catholic community so that all its members will have Christian compassion for those whose marriages have ended in divorce, will appreciate more deeply the holiness and indissolubility of Christian marriage, and respect the need to resolve such cases in the external forum, if possible, whether by the present procedure or by another procedure in which the judgment of the community of believers be expressed. No more should be required of Catholics than what is certainly required by divine institution, as seen in the light of the full Christian tradition of the East as well as the West, and no one should be excluded from ecclesiastical and sacramental Communion unless this is proved to be an absolute demand of divine law.[36]

But perhaps even more thoroughgoing reform is required in marriage tribunal procedure. The responsibility of diocesan tribunals and the regional courts recommended above should be carefully limited, and the judgmental process shifted, for most cases, to the local parish community, in accordance with the principle of subsidiarity. Such a local tribunal would be staffed by the pastor and a board of laypeople. Occasionally, of course, someone might request that his or her marriage actually be declared null, and such petitions could still be handled by the diocesan or regional tribunal. In all tribunal deliberations the traditional *favor juris* granted to the marriage bond should be reversible. Thus, a first marriage would enjoy the benefit of the law so long as there remained some chance of saving it; but the right of a person to enter into a second marriage should enjoy the benefit of the law when it is obvious that the first marriage is beyond repair. No one should be obliged to life-long celibacy on the mere ground of a slight possibility that the previous marriage may have been valid. According to Bernard Häring, there should be no absolute tutiorism militating against the basic human right to marry.[37] When a parish board, therefore, judges that a person is disposed to enter a second marriage "in the Lord," then the marriage would be permitted in the Church. But where it is judged otherwise and the person went through a ceremony anyway, outside the Church, then a second judgment would have to be made regarding the worthiness of that person to receive the Eucharist. All of these judgments would be pastoral in character. The judges would truly be "ministers of reconciliation."[38]

10. WOMEN IN THE CHURCH

It is being said that the Church, and particularly the Catholic Church, is the last major institution in the Western world still dominated by the philosophy and spirit of male chauvinism. Women are positively and completely excluded from every position of official ecclesiastical leadership. It is still widely assumed within the Church that, before God, women are inherently inferior to men.

Accordingly, this radical inequity must be abolished in a way that is at once decisive and pedagogically direct: by admitting women to ordination to the diaconate, the priesthood, and the episcopacy. Such a course would simply reflect the growing consensus among theologians of Catholic and Protestant traditions alike that there is no insurmountable biblical or dogmatic obstacle to the ordination of women and that ordination of women must come to be part of the Church's life. Thus, qualified women should be given full and equal participation in policy- and decision-making, and voice in places of power, in the churches on local, regional, national, and international levels. Seminary education in all the churches should be opened to qualified women, and such women should, of course, be admitted to ordination. In the meantime, the pertinent ecclesiastical agencies (e.g., North American Area Council, World Alliance of Reformed Churches, and the Bishops' Committee on Ecumenical and Interreligious Affairs) should establish and fund an Ecumenical Commission on Women, inviting all churches to join with them on an equal basis in responsibility and funding for this commission and in sharing the fruits of its labors.[39] In the end, it is of the utmost importance that once women are admitted to ordination they not be forced into patterns of ministry that have been developed with a view to an exclusively male clergy.[40]

11. RENEWAL OF RELIGIOUS COMMUNITIES

Religious orders are institutions within an institution. All the problems that beset the Church as a whole affect each of these particular groups in much the same way. Therefore, what has been recommended to the whole Church is to be recommended to these specialized groups within the Church. There is another dimension to religious orders, however, beyond their reality as churches within the Church. In their original inception, these communities functioned as prophetic agents within, but also over against, the rest of the Church. They came into being in response to missionary needs that were no longer being fulfilled properly. Their apostolates not only met those needs, but exercised a prophetic judgment upon the rest of the Church in the process. Today, however, many of these religious communities have become defenders of the old order rather than harbingers of the new. Instead of summoning the whole Church along the path of self-determination and thereby toward continued growth in Christ, these groups often tend to fortify and stiffen the Church in its penchant for the way of tenacity. At the other extreme, smaller groups within some of the orders, in a frenetic reaction against the establishment's tenacity, may have confused elasticity with self-determination.

Accordingly, particular religious communities (some of which may remain attached to orders) must become once again prophetic agents within the Church Universal. They should serve as models of what we have called self-determination and participative management.

Within the religious communities themselves, the members must be provided with all those modern benefits which enlightened social progress sees as basic for one's well-being, but, even more importantly, they must have the opportunity of participating in those decisions which are determinative of their own lives. The communities should reemphasize their solidarity with the poor of the world. There should be a renewed sense of accountability for the resources of the community. Fraternal support and encouragement must be given to those members of the community engaged in the apostolates for peace and justice.

Within the institutions which many of these communities

direct, there should be just wages, adequate working conditions, adequate social security benefits to all employees, irrespective of race, creed, color, or sex. There should be full cooperation with such programs as Project Equality and particular concern for the rights of women at every level. Finally, in the many educational institutions staffed by religious groups, the students must be challenged repeatedly to be outstanding in their commitment to justice, and the schools themselves must be credible signs of this commitment.

Within the Church, these communities must become a public voice, calling the Church to practice justice unstintingly. They must call for austerity in the life-style of the whole Church. They must urge the fullest possible participation by the membership of the Church in decision-making, including the selection of leadership. They should urge a renewed sense of accountability of the resources of the Church. And they should work for full equality in the exercise of the rights of women.

Within the larger human community, religious communities must speak out on issues of peace and justice and involve themselves in movements to correct injustices. They should press for a foreign policy which shifts a government's priorities away from concern for military dominance. They should try to develop a coherent religious voice to heighten the consciousness of the nation in terms of its real impact on the world and to call attention to the gap between that impact and Christian responsibility.[41]

12. THE MINISTRY OF THE ORDAINED

The crisis in the Catholic priesthood is already well known. There is widespread dissatisfaction among the clergy with the exercise of ecclesiastical authority and with the rigid enforcement of traditional life-styles.[42] The thousands of priests who have resigned, and continue to resign, from the active ministry over the last several years is evidence enough of the depth and extent of this dissatisfaction, but the sharp decline in candidates for the ministry and the clergy's indifference to vocational recruitment are even more ominous indications of what is happening.[43]

Accordingly, the Church must recognize the need for a pluriformity of ministerial life-styles and for drawing these ministers more fully into the decision-making process. There are three basic principles that must be translated into practice: the collegial character of the Christian priesthood; the principle of subsidiarity; and the fact that priests have the same personal rights as any other member of the Church.[44]

In the United States today the principal source of conflict and dissatisfaction among Catholic priests is the manner by which authority is exercised within the Church. Unilateral decisions, emanating from a monarchical understanding of the Church, must yield to truly consultative and even deliberative decision-making. Such consultation is not based on any concession or privilege. It is derived, as we have seen earlier, from the nature of the Church itself and from the conviction that the gifts of the Spirit are available to all. Consultation, however, is not achieved when the process is secret to the extent that each person expresses his opinion in isolation from others. Furthermore, there is nothing in the law of the Church to prevent bishops from changing the consultative character of the votes of councils into deliberative or decisive votes. On the contrary, a recent statement of the Vatican's Congregation for the Clergy allowed that priests' councils could not function as deliberative bodies "unless the universal law of the Church provides otherwise or the bishop in individual cases judges it opportune to attribute a deliberative vote to the council."[45] There should be care, however, that the priests' senate does not become a competitive agency alongside or over against the diocesan pastoral council. Conflicts should be resolved by dialogue and by the joint consideration of questions. Disharmony might be avoided if these two councils were made in effect a bicameral consultative or deliberative organ. It would be preferable, however, that the diocesan pastoral council should function as the diocesan policy-making body, and that priests themselves have some representation on that council. Meanwhile, the priests' senates could serve as a forum for the expression of concerns of special interest to the clergy, and its deliberations might, in turn, be submitted to the diocesan pastoral council for consideration. However that issue is to be resolved, it is essential that priests, and others in the diocese, have some meaningful role in the selection of ecclesiastical leadership.

Priests who wish to leave their diocese and engage in the ministry elsewhere should be free to do so. The bishop should not deny permission without a showing of grave necessity in his own diocese. As a corollary of this principle, bishops should not refuse permission to priests or deacons for service in their dioceses without just cause, such as a showing of grave unworthiness, incompetence, or a lack of real need in that diocese. Canon 144 provides clearly that an ordained minister should not be recalled to his diocese without just cause and that the requirements of natural equity should always be observed. Bishops may not arbitrarily recall their priests from other dioceses, but they should welcome their voluntary return to the service of the diocese of their incardination. At present, violations of these rights can be remedied only by recourse to the Vatican. Priests and deacons must be given the opportunity of recourse to regional or national administrative tribunals for speedy redress of wrongs.

In principle it should be agreed that the ordained minister has the same rights and freedoms as the other members of the Church, except as these may be extended or limited by the legitimate needs of the ministry he exercises. The ordained minister should have the right to resign from the exercise of the ministry formally acknowledged in ecclesiastical law. Nothing further, beyond a resignation submitted to the bishop, should be demanded of him. Employment by a church or church-

related organization should not be denied those who have resigned from the active ministry.

With regard to pastoral ministries, the Vatican II decree on
the pastoral office of bishops in the Church and the apostolic
letter implementing it provide a broad base for experimenta-
tion, adaptation, and creative innovation in parish structures.
The bishop is clearly empowered to innovate, without restriction, for the good of souls. This would include the establishment
of "team ministries," "floating parishes," student communities,
professional or occupational groupings, etc. The only necessary
elements for a parish are an identifiable community and a stable
pastoral office; determined buildings or defined territory are of
secondary importance and nonconstitutive.

The principal criterion for continuation in the ministerial
office should be effective performance, reviewed at regular intervals. Among the criteria to be employed are: competence in
liturgical celebration, effective preaching, genuine social concern, ability to lead (to clarify the goals of the Church and to
motivate people to pursue them), ecumenical sensitivity, and
skill in pastoral counseling. Continuing education of the clergy
remains a matter of highest importance. Why is it, Richard
Dillon asks, that "suddenly, in the laicization process, the
church adopts a policy of stern scrutiny such as was never enforced in the priest's recruitment and formation! The high
ideals of priestly formation set forth in the encyclicals and curial
instructions stand in ludicrous contrast to the practice of most
seminaries, where a shortage of numbers dictates the collapse
of standards and an uneducated, undisciplined clergy emerges
to minister to an increasingly impatient laity."[46]

Vatican II acknowledged that the obligation of clerical celibacy derives from a law of the Church, not from a law of God.
The council also affirmed that the right to marry is "universal
and inviolable."[47] Consequently, sacred orders should no
longer be regarded as a diriment impediment to marriage. The
right to marry, as an inviolable and universal right, must always

remain in the disposition of the person. Since this change will eventually come about, the leadership should begin now to prepare the general membership of the whole Church so that they will easily, and for the right reasons, accept a married clergy.

13. ECUMENICAL RELATIONSHIPS

The ecumenical movement has faltered so noticeably in recent years that articles have begun to appear asking if we are now in a postecumenical era or whether we have simply reached an impasse in the quest for Christian unity.[48] On the Protestant side, resistance and especially apathy have stalled the forward thrust of the Consultation on Church Union (COCU); on the Catholic side, there has been a tightening of regulations governing intercommunion and a stubbornly silent rejection of proposals for some mutual recognition of ministries. The desire to maintain institutional integrity (the way of tenacity) accounts for much of the resistance on the Protestant side; and devotion to a particular notion of apostolic succession accounts for much of the resistance on the Catholic side, particularly among the leadership.

Accordingly, the Catholic Church will have to accept the implications of its own conciliar teaching that the Body of Christ embraces non-Catholic Christians as well as Catholics, the varying degrees of incorporation into the Church notwithstanding. This will require an official endorsement of intercommunion on some limited basis and also a public acceptance of the validity of some non-Catholic ordained ministries. Meanwhile, the results of the various bilateral conversations that have been taking place in the United States since 1965 must be disseminated more widely and more effectively than heretofore. The primary responsibility for publicity should probably be assigned to the ecumenical officers and commissions of the individual denominations and eventually to an ecumenical board which would oversee and coordinate the consultations in the United States with one another, with consultations in other nations, and with the international dialogues. This agency might also sponsor on occasion trilateral and multilateral conversations as was done, for example, in the case of the National Council of Churches (NCC) consultation on the Eucharist in 1970. Such an ecumenical board might be placed under the aegis of the Faith and Order Commission of the NCC, provided that such a step would not be unacceptable to those communions which are not now members of Faith and Order. Beyond what such an ecumenical board might accomplish by way of coordination and publicity, the responsible agencies of the various churches should take steps to ensure that the clergy and laity are kept informed of the theological developments taking place in the consultations. The dialogues could profitably be presented for study in episcopal seminars (which might well be ecumenical in composition), diocesan clergy conferences (to which clergy of other denominations might appropriately be invited), adult education programs, and popular literature.

Furthermore, these consultation reports must be followed up with appropriate formal action by the churches involved. The normal practice thus far in the Catholic Church has been for the National Conference of Catholic Bishops to receive the reports and forward them to the Papal Secretariat for the Promotion of Christian Unity. Beyond this, the bishops should sponsor further studies, publicize the areas of doctrinal agreement, and give appropriate pastoral directives. In the absence of some implementation of the principles accepted by the bilateral groups, the gap between theological discussion and pastoral practice will widen to the point where the value of further discussion will inevitably be challenged on all sides.

The consultations themselves might be elevated in quality by a better selection process for their members. Professional societies within the Church (e.g., the Catholic Theological Society of America, the Canon Law Society of America, or the Catholic

Biblical Association) might be requested formally to make recommendations of qualified theologians and of those whose academic disciplines are of immediate concern to theology. No qualified scholar, even though he be someone who has resigned from the active ministry, should be excluded from these dialogue groups.[49]

In the last several years the Catholic Church has joined many metropolitan and state councils of churches and has become a member of the Faith and Order Commission on both the national and the world level. The possibility of Catholic membership in the National Council of Churches and the World Council of Churches is being actively considered. Such steps are already long overdue, even though they will not necessarily produce dramatic results in themselves.[50]

The most serious practical problem with the ecumenical movement today is that it remains essentially the concern of specialists. Until the rank-and-file membership perceives the importance and relevance of ecumenism to their own Christian lives, it will tend to remain stalled in its own tracks. True motivation for mission, as I have argued earlier in the chapter, requires that the individual members of the Church be able to identify the organizational objectives with their own personal objectives.

Theological Arguments and Counterarguments

1. PRINCIPLES OF CONSTITUTIONALISM

Objections are raised against the principle of constitutionalism in the Church: *(a)* since the authority of the Church is divine, it cannot be limited, held accountable, nor is it subject to correction; *(b)* the executive, legislative, and judicial power must converge in a single individual because the Church is, by divine institution, an absolute monarchy; *(c)* any other system would constitute a betrayal not only of the will of Christ but also of the Church's own entire history and tradition.

The first two objections flow from a naïve and narrow theology of history. The first objection makes two assumptions: that the Church and the hierarchy are one and the same (thus "authority of the *Church*" is made equivalent to "authority of the *hierarchy*"); and that the Church has, for all practical purposes, no significantly human element at all. The first assumption cannot be demonstrated. On the contrary, the Second Vatican Council clearly distinguishes between hierarchy and Church; the former is in the service of the latter. The Church, on the other hand, is the whole People of God, and this includes laity, religious, and clergy alike.[51] The second assumption applies the same kind of thinking to the Church as was once applied to Christ himself. From the earliest days of the Church, there were Christians who could not maintain a proper balance between the humanity and the divinity of Jesus. Some emphasized the humanity at the expense of the divinity (Adoptionism, Arianism, etc.) and others—the more widespread tendency—emphasized the divinity at the expense of the humanity (Docetism, Monophysitism, etc.).[52] One cannot speak about the Church as if it were so thoroughly divine that only the slightest and most inconsequential items can be regarded as human and therefore subject to change (e.g., whether olive oil or vegetable oil may be used for the anointing of the sick, whether Catholics shall eat meat on Friday, etc.). Such a view assumes, at a deeper level, that the Church and the Kingdom of God are identical (a position impossible to sustain biblically, doctrinally, or theologically) and that the idea of a substantial reform of the Church is always without merit (a view contradicted in practice, not only by Vatican II, but by such earlier thoroughgoing renovations as the Gregorian Reform of the eleventh century). Indeed, if the Church were not so constitutively human as it is divine, it could not be called a mystery or a sacrament, just as the earlier denials of the integral humanity of Jesus had the effect of undermining his role as a sacrament of encounter with God and, therefore, of redemption.[53]

Neither can the second objection to the principle of constitutionalism be demonstrated. Even though it may have been an assumption commonly held and circulated among Catholics for most of the twentieth century, the belief that the Church is, by the will of Christ, an absolute monarchy is simply without biblical, doctrinal, or theological foundation. On the contrary, the teaching of the Second Vatican Council on the collegiality of the Church is irreconcilable with the notion of absolute monarchy. The position paper issued by the Canon Law Society's symposium on "Unity and Subsidiarity in the Church" (September 1969) synthesizes the counterargument:

Collegiality is, in its first and deepest meaning, a matter of *community*. The Church is a *communio* brought together and sustained by the Holy Spirit. The Church, as community, comes into being in its most visible form when it gathers for the celebration of the Eucharist, at the level of the local assembly. But this local church is not merely an administrative unit within a larger corporate entity; it is a living cell containing the whole mystery of the one Body of Christ. Within these local churches, there has always existed a close bond among bishops, presbyters and deacons, and the community as a whole, and this fraternal relationship is a principal basis for the apostolicity of each community.

There have also existed important links among the various local churches: bishop with bishop, and community with community. It is clear from very early liturgical testimony (e.g., the consecration of a bishop by several other bishops rather than by one alone), that the individual bishop could have his episcopacy in no other way than in communion with the other bishops. The Church is a *communio ecclesiarum*, a fraternity of local churches brought together by the Spirit into a single body. The history of the Catholic Church, in large measure, is the record of balancing one value against the other, of preserving the integrity of the local church (apostolicity) without diminishing the unity of the Church universal (catholicity).

The mission of the Church, whether of proclaiming the Word of God, of celebrating the sacraments, or of ministering to the needs of mankind in the world for the sake of the Kingdom of God, presupposes and requires both order and structure, not only as a sign of internal unity but also for a more coherent and effective exercise of this mission. The unity of the Church and the fruitfulness of its mission is assured interiorly by the presence of the Spirit, and exteriorly by the presence of the college of bishops within the Church, and by the pope as the principle of unity within the college.

The pope, however, never acts as a purely private person when he acts as head of the Church. He is always head of the college and a member thereof. The primacy of the pope is a primacy within rather than over against the episcopal college. The Church is governed by a college in such wise that the pope is not the mere instrument of the college, while the college is not merely his executive organ. Indeed, the Catholic Church does not recognize the pope to be its absolute monarch, nor the bishops as the mere delegates of the pope. The supreme and full power for governing the Church, in view of its higher mission for the sake of the Kingdom of God, has been conferred upon the whole college. This power is exercised in different modes and forms, but it is radically one.

It was clearly not the intent of the First Vatican Council to propose a doctrine of the papacy that might be prejudicial to the rights and responsibilities of the bishops. This judgment is verified by the joint Declaration of the German Hierarchy in 1875. Herein it is asserted that the council did not teach that episcopal jurisdiction is absorbed into papal jurisdiction or that the pope in principle has taken the place of every individual bishop. Significantly, Pope Pius IX approved this statement of the German bishops as expressing "the true meaning of the Vatican decrees" and preventing the faithful from "forming a false idea of them."

This interpretation is further strengthened by the documents of the Second Vatican Council. Without prejudice to the rights and preroga- tives of the pope, "all the bishops in hierarchical communion share in the responsibility for the Universal Church" (Decree on the Bishops' Pastoral Office in the Church, n. 5), and are thereby "the subject of supreme and full power over the universal Church" (Dogmatic Consti- tution on the Church, n. 22).

The testimony of Vatican II faithfully reflects the converging in- sights of biblical, liturgical, canonical, and theological scholarship: the Church must be collegial in structure and government because it is collegial in its nature and origins, and history records numerous exam- ples of collegial action in every age of the Church's life.[54]

The third objection is historical rather than theological, and it is even more easily refuted. The institutional pluralism of the New Testament Church is now so universally acknowledged by biblical scholars and theologians of every Christian tradition that the burden of proof for a divinely intended monarchical structure, indeed an absolutely monarchical structure, rests entirely upon the shoulders of those who want to persist in that view.[55] Indeed, church historians recognize that "for the first 250 years of its history the Christian Church was far from being a highly centralized institution."[56] And constitutionalism itself has its roots in the Catholic Church's own medieval experience.[57]

2. DECENTRALIZATION OF POWER

Objections to the decentralization of power and the conferring of deliberative authority and organizational independence upon such bodies as parish councils and diocesan pastoral councils are based on the same assumptions outlined above. Such objections are correctly associated with those Catholics whose understanding of the Church follows the Theory A pattern. However, there are other Catholics who, while no longer accepting the Theory A view, cannot support the proposal that councils within the Church be given deliberative power. The Theory B Catholic believes in the principles of consultation, of subsidiarity, and of collegiality. He does not regard the Pope or the bishop as an absolute monarch who may or may not enter the consultation process, as he may desire. Nevertheless, the role of the ordained leader is of such importance for the integrity of the Church that nothing can be allowed to encroach upon that role to such an extent that the role itself might become indistinguishable from other ministries and, therefore, expendable. Such an objection rests upon a misunderstanding of the nature of deliberative, as opposed to consultative, power. Deliberative authority does not preclude distinctive executive leadership. Legislative assemblies in democratic countries are deliberative bodies, but their decisions can be overruled by executive action (the veto). However, such executive action must itself be subject to review (either by the overriding of the veto by a much larger majority, or by judicial decree); otherwise that executive prerogative is monarchical in essence.

Moreover, the present disciplinary decrees of the Catholic Church permit in principle the granting of deliberative authority to given conciliar bodies. The recent statement of the Vatican's Congregation for the Clergy (April 11, 1970), to which I have already referred, concedes that priests' councils may not enact decisions which bind the bishop (a binding decision implies deliberative power, of course), "unless the universal law of the Church provides otherwise or the bishop in individual cases judges it opportune to attribute a deliberative vote to the council."[58]

3. Planning and Research

Objections to the establishment of offices of planning and research, financial management, public opinion, and public relations are based more tangentially on theological assumptions. But insofar as theological principles are at the root of such opposition, these principles are fundamentally the same as were at issue in the debate about constitutionalism (see p. 108ff., above). Positively, the proposals for the creation of such offices reflect the theological conviction that the Church includes all baptized Christians, that all of the Church's membership, therefore, are responsible for its mission, and that if they are to be effective in carrying out that missionary responsibility, they will require all the information and data that can practically be gathered.

4. Principles of Accountability

Objections to the establishment of a completely independent adversary agency within the Church would follow the same pattern as outlined above. The positive argument for such an agency would be essentially the same as given in section 3, above; namely, that the importance of the Church's mission demands that it be planned and executed as carefully and as effectively as possible. Theologically, the community engaged in mission is a sinful as well as holy people.[59] A realistic response to this abiding element of sinfulness and the proclivity thereto requires the kind of institution suggested herein.

5. SELECTION OF BISHOPS

Objections to the widening of the episcopal selection process are based on two assumptions, one theological and one practical: *(a)* that the Pope alone has the right to appoint bishops, because he is the Church's absolute monarch and bishops are only his delegates or vicars; and *(b)* that no electoral system, apart from the present method, could work. The theological assumption has already been considered in the first and subsequent items.[60] The second, practical assumption reflects again a remarkably narrow view of history. There were, in fact, other systems, from the earliest days of the Church. Indeed, the present system, which allows no voice for the clergy and people of a community, is the one without real historical precedent.[61] It was after the sixth century that the Church came under the domination of lay princes who largely determined promotions to the episcopate, since bishops were by now deeply involved in secular politics and in the administration of both property and secular jurisdiction. The Gregorian reform movement attempted to eliminate lay domination and to restore election by "clergy and people" *(clerus et populus)*, but in the twelfth century elections increasingly became the exclusive prerogative of the cathedral clergy, while the laity was limited to a mere right of passive consent. It was in the thirteenth century that the papacy first intruded itself in the selection process by intervening more and more in the confirmation, translation, and provision (i.e., by direct appointment) of bishops to dioceses. Both the transition to election by the cathedral clergy and the transition to papal intervention were prompted by the turbulence of the previous electoral process and by the frequency of contested elections. It was the Council of Trent which systematized the papal prerogative in the selection of bishops.

From the earliest times, too, the bishop's position derived from the community which had elected him and his authority derived directly from Christ. In modern canonical terms, this authority was regarded as fully and truly "ordinary jurisdiction." Beginning in the period from the eleventh to the thirteenth centuries, however, episcopal jurisdiction was increasingly regarded as immediately derivative from the Holy See. From the Council of Trent to Vatican II, in the exercise of his jurisdictional authority, the bishop acted either as the chosen agent of the Roman See or of the secular power, or of both.

Therefore, according to ecclesiastical and canonical historians, it is clear that at any moment after the sixth century, with the exception of the brief Gregorian revival (late eleventh and early twelfth centuries), bishops were no longer selected by a process which adequately expressed the community's consent and represented the community's will. Thus the close relation between bishop and community—so characteristic of the early Church—gradually weakened.

In the twentieth century one no longer finds the most crucial factors which made electoral participation of the laity impractical. The laity are no longer uneducated or illiterate, and they are far more disciplined than, say, in the twelfth century. Nor is the Church so involved in the political and economic life of society requiring the intimate involvement of political leaders in the selection process.[62] On the contrary. In those states where the practice once flourished even in our own time, such as Spain, the Church is now disengaging itself from such alliances.

Theologically, since every baptized Christian is a member of the People of God and shares in that People's mission, and since the ordained leadership of the Church exists for the sake of leading and directing the People of God in the fulfillment of its mission, it follows that the larger community—laity, religious, and clergy alike—should participate in some meaningful way in the process whereby these ordained leaders are selected. This theology is entirely in accord with the ancient canonical principle that "he who governs all should be elected by all."

6. PAPAL POWER

Objections to *(a)* the Pope's sharing of supreme governing authority with an International Synod of Bishops, *(b)* the decentralization of authority away from the Vatican, and *(c)* the imposing of limitations on the papal office by regulating the term of office and widening the process of selecting the office-holder are based on several familiar assumptions: that the Church is an absolute monarchy; that local churches, or dioceses, are only administrative units of a monolithic organization governed from the top; and that the designation of the Pope, the key to the whole ecclesiastical organization, must be made by a process that will best reflect the divine origin of, and involvement in, that designation process.

The first assumption has already been considered. It is wholly without merit. The second assumption betrays a radical misunderstanding of the meaning of collegiality. The Church is essentially a *communio ecclesiarum,* a fraternity of local churches brought together into a single body by the Spirit. The whole Church is, in one sense, embodied in each local expression thereof, and yet that local community is not really a living cell within the Body of Christ unless it is somehow in communion with all of the other local communities. The collegial nature of the Church requires some balance between the demands of unity, on the one hand, and the demands of local sovereignty (guaranteed by the principle of subsidiarity), on the other. A concentration of all meaningful authority in the papal administration may protect the universal character of the Church, but it submerges its collegial character. The assumption, i.e., that dioceses are only administrative units of the Church itself, is a product of bad ecclesiology. It is insupportable by ecclesiastical doctrine, particularly the teaching of the Second Vatican Council.[63]

The third assumption is politically as well as theologically naïve. By granting the right of election to the College of Cardinals, which by primitive Christian standards must be regarded as an innovation itself, the Church has already conceded the principle that the Pope can have title to his office only after he has been designated officially by a more or less representative group within the total membership. The weakness in the system whereby the Pope is elected by cardinals only is that they are themselves designees, by unilateral action, of previous Popes. Members of an international synod, on the other hand, are elected to that body by their brother bishops in their own countries. If the episcopal selection process were also to change, then the selection of synodal members would be even more representative.

7. EPISCOPAL POWER

Objections to the election of bishops according to a wider, more representative, and more public process have already been raised in connection with the fourth proposal, above (p. 113f.). Resistance to the proposal that dioceses be governed, not by the bishop alone, but by the diocesan pastoral council over which the bishop presides, is similarly based on an assumption already considered; namely, that the Church is monarchical in structure, that bishops serve, at the pleasure of the Pope, as monarchs within their own dioceses, and, finally, that the mission of the Church is given directly only to Peter, the apostles, and their successors. The proposal that bishops not be allowed to impose restrictions over their own communities when such restrictions are not imposed on other communities of similar composition and circumstances is resisted on the grounds that a bishop is supreme in his own diocese (a point that we have already challenged in several different ways) and that his only real allegiance is to the Pope. This latter assumption again distorts the collegial dimension of the Church. Indeed, it also violates the canonical principal, *Odiosa restringi sunt* (restrictions are to be applied to the least amount of persons and situations). The relation of the bishop and his diocese to the rest of the Church is not only mediated vertically through the Pope and the See of Rome, but also horizontally through communion with all of the other local communities who, in turn, are united with the Pope and the See of Rome. It is wholly incorrect, therefore, to suggest that an individual Catholic's responsibility of obedience (in an official, not evangelical, sense) is to his own bishop and to the Pope. The consensus views of the bishops of a given region or nation are also of concern to the Catholic. Indeed, the authority of a regional or national episcopal conference would have to be greater than that of an individual bishop. Thus, if a matter is accepted by a national conference (e.g., as in the case of due process), it is wholly unjustifiable that it not be an option for church members in every diocese within that conference. This is in keeping with the canonical principle, *Favores convenit ampliari sunt* (favors are to be as broadly distributed as possible). Finally, opposition to a restriction on the translation of bishops from one diocese to another would seem to reflect sheerly political views of the Church and its offices rather than a particular theological understanding of the nature of the Church. Those who look upon the office of bishop as a rung in a careerist's promotional ladder totally distort the nature of the episcopal ministry, and characterizing one diocese as small and unattractive and another diocese as large and prestigious is completely contrary to the whole theology of the local church. To suggest that one diocese is something less than another because of quantitative factors of this sort would be as theologically dubious as to suggest that a small piece of the eucharistic bread contains less of Christ than does a large piece.

Much of the bishop's exaggerated self-image, and particularly his view of himself as the "one teacher" of a given diocese, can be attributed to a mechanical, chronologically oriented understanding of apostolic succession which still enjoys wide currency throughout much of the Catholic Church. Even newly appointed auxiliary bishops, in their euphoric moment of barely disguised self-congratulation laden with protestations of unworthiness and surprise, are prone to define themselves as "successors of the apostles." There is already something ecclesiologically dubious about the very "office" of auxiliary bishop,[64] but even if one were to understand that ecclesiastical rank as truly and fully episcopal, one would still have to challenge the "successor of the apostles" description. A bishop is not himself a successor of the apostles. At most, a bishop is, by episcopal ordination, introduced into the college of bishops which, in turn, understands itself as being in continuity with the college of the apostles.

But even this notion of apostolic succession is vulnerable to radical criticism. Recent New Testament scholarship has tended to undermine many of the key assumptions of Theory A regarding apostolic succession. There are presbyter-bishops in the New Testament that were not in any traceable way the successors of the twelve apostles. Indeed, it is quite plausible that when churches without presbyter-bishops ultimately established them, they did so in imitation of churches that already had them, but many times without specific apostolic appointment. "The affirmation," Raymond Brown suggests in the light of this evidence, "that the episcopate was divinely established or established by Christ himself can be defended in the nuanced sense that the episcopate gradually emerged in a Church that stemmed from Christ and that this emergence was (in the eyes of faith) guided by the Holy Spirit."[65] In any case, the twelve apostles and the missionary apostles eventually disappeared from the primitive ecclesiastical scene, and many of their functions were taken over by the bishops who remained. The New Testament, Brown argues, simply does not give us much evidence about the transition from a Church where the apostles ranked first to a Church where the bishops ranked first, "but if we read between the lines of III John we have an interesting indication that the transition was not always smooth."[66]

Apostolic succession is better applied to the whole Church rather than to any particular ministerial group or single official within that Church. It means that the Church as a whole is committed to obedience to the apostles as the original witnesses and the original messengers. The Church as a whole is successor to the apostles insofar as it remains bound to the word, the witness, and the service of the first apostolic generation. Apostolic succession, therefore, is primarily a succession in apostolic faith, apostolic service, and apostolic life. There may also be successions of offices, but it would be wrong to suggest that the only offices in apostolic succession are the papacy and the episcopacy. There are also a succession of prophets and a succession of teachers.[67] Raising the issue of a succession of teachers opens one of the most emotional debates in the contemporary Catholic Church, on the relative authority of bishops and theologians. There are bishops who, for some mysteriously perverse reason, delight in assuring their audiences that theologians have absolutely no official or authoritative standing in the Church. What theologians say and write is strictly a matter of their own personal opinion, to be taken with no greater seriousness than, let us say, the gruff fulminations of a pastor in a Sunday pulpit—perhaps even with less seriousness. This view cannot be sustained, even biblically. New Testament scholar Myles Bourke has written:

If there is any group in the Church which has the right to be heard when the Church makes decisions, it is that composed of those to whom the charism of teaching has been given, the *didaskaloi,* who, in the list of 1 Cor. 12:28 rank third after the apostles and the prophets. If the charism now exists in the Church apart from the hierarchy—and to deny that it does is utterly arbitrary—it is surely possessed by the theologians. If the "whole Church" is to have a part in the making of decisions, particularly in the making of decisions which bear upon the content of faith, the proper authority of the theologians must be given much more weight than is often the case in the present functioning of the Church.[68]

8. A BILL OF RIGHTS

Objections to the proposal for a bill of rights in the Church originate from the notion that the Church is a divinely in-stituted monarchy, not a democracy, and that it is a *societas perfecta*, not a pilgrim people. These assumptions have already been explored and criticized earlier in this chapter. Positively, freedom is essential to Christian life because it is a life in the Spirit, and "where the Spirit of the Lord is, there is freedom" (2 Cor. 3:17). The Christian, who lives in the Spirit, cannot allow his life to be governed by the purely external restraint of law. Christian moral living is not a means of acquiring the Spirit, but the fruit of possessing God's free gift of the Spirit; it is a response to grace. The observance of law does not constitute a person a child of God; rather, what is required is obedience to the unique "law of Christ," the law of love. Radical freedom is total free-dom, but it is not absolute. Man remains capable of sin, of trampeling upon the freedoms of his brothers and sisters. The specification of Christian freedom (as in a bill of rights) is neces-sary for the mutual protection of one another's freedom. Unfor-tunately, the regulations and procedures of the modern Code of Canon Law, which itself "reflects both the Church's heritage of Roman law and the mood of intense, inward-looking defen-siveness that characterized the Tridentine age," are "often inappropriate to the life of the modern world [and] in some spheres they are shackling the liberty of the Christian peo-ple."[69]

9. ECCLESIASTICAL COURTS

Objections to proposed reforms of marriage courts, and other ecclesiastical courts, also reflect an understanding of the Church as a *societas perfecta*, without institutional spot or wrinkle, unaccountable to its own membership for its procedures and performance. The reluctance to accept internal-forum solutions to certain marriage cases only underlines a predominantly institutional attitude toward the Church. Solutions in the internal forum preclude, or at least circumvent, the external forum process. What is not decided in the external forum is thereby removed from the power and control of the leadership. Since the way of paternalism (over against even the way of scientific management or, certainly, of participative management) is Theory A's principal, if not exclusive, method of motivation, and since, on the other hand, the way of tenacity (over against the way of elasticity or the way of self-determination) is Theory A's principal, if not exclusive, approach to institutional change, it is not entirely surprising that objections would be raised, first, against any real change of the tribunal system and, second, against yielding more control to the individuals directly involved in marriage problems. I have already discussed the ecclesiological difficulties attendant upon both underlying approaches: the way of paternalism and the way of tenacity. Those same ecclesiological assumptions are operative here. Opposition to procedural reform is also based on a limited understanding of the historical data. It is simply assumed that divorce-and-remarriage was never possible according to the theology and jurisprudence of the Church. There is a second view, however, which insists, on the basis of both theology and history, that remarriage after divorce can sometimes be permitted. This latter view is called the "fragility-illiceity tradition," i.e., it recognizes the marriage bond as breakable, under certain extreme conditions, and acknowledges that a second marriage after divorce can be valid, although illicit. This second tradition, according to Lawrence Wrenn, is "an ancient and honorable one endorsed by popes and saints and bishops and fathers of the Church over extended periods of time."[70] He argues, furthermore, that the alternative to reviving this tradition is "meaning-less and dysfunctional." Our present tribunal system is in quick-sand and sinking more deeply every day.

Positively, the Church is called to be a sign of the Kingdom of God, where justice and charity abide. Where justice is delayed, justice is denied. Where charity is regulated and con-trolled in every detail, for every conceivable situation, charity gives way to legalism. In any case, no burden is to be imposed "beyond what is indispensable" (Acts 15:28). The burden of proving indispensability is always upon those who wish to im-pose burdens in the first place.

10. WOMEN IN THE CHURCH

Objections against the ordination of women are reducible to two: (a) Christ, the High Priest, was himself a man; and (b) Neither Christ, nor the apostles, nor any bishops in the post-apostolic Church ever ordained, or sanctioned the ordination of, women.

The maleness of Jesus is as much a part of his limited human condition as were his Jewishness, his Aramaic speech, his birth in Palestine. There is absolutely no biblical, doctrinal, or theo-logical basis for suggesting that his maleness was a necessary precondition for the Incarnation; or, conversely, that female-ness is intrinsically opposed to the nature of God; or, indeed, that God is a sexual being in the first instance. The second objection is more serious. It argues that because the Church has never done a certain thing, the Church can never do it. First, it ignores the cultural circumstances in which Christ and his original disciples found themselves. The selection of women as apostles or as major officials in the early Church would have violated the incarnational principle. In other words, we should have been just as surprised to have found women bishops in the earliest years of the Church as we should have been to have found marriage tribunals, chancery offices, a Roman Curia, a

Code of Canon Law, a Latin Eucharist, papal appointment of bishops, apostolic delegates, benediction, Eucharistic Congresses, the rosary, papal encyclicals, religious orders, clerical celibacy, Marian devotion, cathedrals, the granting of indulgences, cardinals, monsignors, or curates. Each of these items began at some point *after* the foundational period, and many of them *long* after. The same argument could have been applied to each of them: "We've never done it before!" Someone might then be tempted to argue that the ordination of women is different because the nonpractice has been in force from the very beginning. But again that argument could have been applied to each of the exemplary items before any of them was first introduced. Furthermore, if one truly believes in the "this worldly" permanence of the Church, and if one acknowledges that this world may continue to exist for thousands and thousands of years more (if we do not choke ourselves to death in the meantime), then historians of the far-distant future may include this period of ours with "the early Church" and note approvingly how so many innovations, including the ordination of women, occurred during this time of ecclesiastical infancy and childhood!

Opponents of the ordination of women have rigorously universalized the Pauline prohibitions in 1 Cor. 14:33–36 (". . . the women should keep silence in the churches . . .") far beyond its context, but they have not been equally rigorous with Gal. 3:28 (". . . there is neither male nor female . . ."), "a verse which admits the ministry of women as clearly as any biblical passage admits anything."[71] But Paul was a Jew and as a Jew he could not accept women as full religious persons. Paul rose above his Judaism in Gal. 3:28, but that he did not always remain at the level to which he rose is attested to in 1 Cor. 14:33–36. "It is time for the Christian churches to ask whether their ministerial structures have echoed Paul's Judaism or Paul's Christianity."[72]

Having set aside these two standard arguments, we are left with the only real argument operative in this debate: the assumption that, before God, women are inherently inferior to men. That is an argument the Theory A Catholic really ought to develop, if he dares, particularly in the light of the following conciliar declaration:

True, all men are not alike from the point of view of varying physical power and the diversity of intellectual and moral resources. Nevertheless, with respect to fundamental rights of the person, every type of discrimination, whether social or cultural, whether based on sex, race, color, social condition, language, or religion, is to be overcome and eradicated as contrary to God's intent. For in truth it must still be regretted that fundamental personal rights are not yet being universally honored. Such is the case of a woman who is denied the right and freedom to choose a husband, to embrace a state of life, or to acquire an education or cultural benefits equal to those recognized for men.[73]

11. RENEWAL OF RELIGIOUS COMMUNITIES

Opposition to the proposed reforms within religious orders (and *a fortiori* to the frequent suggestions by Gabriel Moran that orders themselves should publicly acknowledge and accept the fact that they are already dead) are based on several related theological assumptions, all of which have been at issue in one or another previous item. Thus: *(a)* the Church is an institution before it is a community, and it is an institution whose response to change must be one of tenacity, if it is to survive, and whose approach to its own members must be one of paternalism, if the organization is to hold together and, ultimately, to survive; *(b)* religious orders are meant to be a comfort and a source of strength to the Church, as the Church itself is called to be a comfort and a source of strength to the world. Challenging the Church, attacking its established policies and leaders, departing from its accepted norms of conduct, is to betray the very trust which the Church has placed in these orders and because of which the Church has granted them a special kind of status within her universal organization; *(c)* authority in the religious order must follow the same monarchical pattern as exists, by divine will, in the Church itself; *(d)* members of religious communities must remain apart from the world, even over against it, just as the Church is called to remain apart from it, and (depending on the circumstances) over against it; and *(e)* emphasis on freedom at the expense of order and discipline is the gateway to wholesale infidelity to one's lifelong commitment to the Lord.

The first objection, as the reader has undoubtedly long since concluded, is the one that runs through practically every controversy in the contemporary Church. The fundamental problem is ecclesiological, i.e., theoretical. Catholics cannot make sense of, not to say accept, various changes and proposals for change because their vision of the Church, however sincerely held, simply will not allow them to understand or embrace such change. These Catholics cannot assimilate the most fundamental ecclesiological truth underlying the Vatican II documents; namely, that the Church is people, and a pilgrim people at that. A people is not an institution. The people may in fact institutionalize its life; indeed such institutionalization is inevitable. But by the very nature of "people," it is impossible to institutionalize every aspect of that life. There is simply too much that escapes the reach of structural scaffolding. There are too many unpredictable, uncontrollable elements in the life of a people. People are alive. Like all living things, people stay alive only insofar as they change. That which changes not at all is dead. A wholly institutional notion of Church carries with it a strong tendency toward the way of tenacity. The Church's response to its changing environment is modeled upon the rock's response to the ocean. It survives, but gradually it is being worn away. And most importantly, the rock cannot grow. Yet the Church is called to growth, even to perfection. The way of tenacity is not only bad institutional policy; it is bad theology. Most objections to changes in religious life, however, spring from this fundamentally institutionalized view of the Church.

The second objection also betrays a truncated, if not distorted, concept of church mission. It assumes that the Church must function, sociologically, as a key part of the cultural establishment. In time of war, it rings the bell for patriotism. In the presence of government officials (e.g., at White House prayer services), it flatters and congratulates. Prophecy, which means the discernment and exposure of the inevitable gaps between the future Kingdom of promise and the present reality we have managed to create for ourselves, is marginalized. The mission of the Church is reduced to word-and-sacrament, contrary to the teaching of Vatican II's Pastoral Constitution on the Church in the Modern World, the Third International Synod of Bishops' decree "Justice in the World," and similar documents of recent years. The religious community, like the Church itself, cannot function only as chaplain and cheerleader; both have at least an equal responsibility to challenge and at times to infuriate their respective environments.

The third objection has already been considered in some detail in the first and subsequent items. This objection also betrays a naïve and insufficient understanding of how and under what circumstances people are motivated to give their best for organizational objectives.

The fourth objection also fails to perceive and accept the constitutively human aspect of the Church. The Church is not out of the world; it is part of the world, indeed it is that part of the world which alone confesses and celebrates the Lordship of Jesus of Nazareth and explicitly associates itself with his missionary responsibility for the coming of the Kingdom of God. It is a view incompatible, for example, with Vatican II's Pastoral Constitution which, pointedly, speaks of the Church *in* the world, not the Church *and* the world.

The fifth objection reflects a misunderstanding of Christian moral responsibility. The same arguments that I have already advanced in the discussion of a bill of rights (section 8, p. 121) are applicable here. Those who fear freedom fear the Holy Spirit.

Positively, the renewal of religious communities can make

them be for the Church what the Church is called to be for the rest of the world: the avant-garde of the Kingdom of God, a showplace, a demonstration community where the power of God's reconciling Spirit is convincingly and, it may be said, reassuringly manifested. A religious community which leaves the Church at peace with its most comforting illusions is as derelict in its missionary duty as a Church which leaves the world untroubled in its antihuman value system. In both relationships it is the Kingdom of God which is at stake.

12. THE MINISTRY OF THE ORDAINED

Objections to the several proposals for reform of the presbyteral ministry spring, again, from the fundamental assumptions about the nature and mission of the Church to which I have already called attention. Specifically, these objections reflect a mistaken understanding of collegiality, too little regard for the principle of subsidiarity, and an exaggerated regard for the status of the ordained minister over against the rest of the Church. Thus, objections to priests' senates by Theory A Catholics rest on the ground that the Church is a monarchical institution and, in a given administrative subdivision of that institution, the bishop functions, at the pleasure of the Pope, with monarchical authority. This assumption has already been considered. Objections to priests' senates by Theory B Catholics arise only when the proposal is offered that such bodies be deliberative as well as consultative in nature. The Theory B Catholic concludes that such a step would go beyond the stated position of Vatican II and would therefore be an unwarranted extension of the conciliar directives. The first response to this objection is that the conciliar texts do not preclude the granting of deliberative power to such consultative bodies. One might reasonably determine this to be, in fact, an implication of the council's teaching on the collegial nature of the Church, and of its insistence that the bishop and his priests share the one priest-

hood of Christ and are united with one another in the fulfillment of their common mission. But even more to the point, the
Vatican itself has sanctioned such a development in the recent
directive from the Congregation for the Clergy, to which I
twice referred above. A bishop may indeed grant deliberative,
decision-making authority to his priests' senate or, it would
follow, to other comparable agencies, if he so desires. The specific proposal in this book is that this *ad hoc* concession be
institutionalized for the ecclesiological reasons already given;
namely, that the mission belongs radically to all and therefore
all must have, at least in principle, some opportunity to participate in the decision-making processes whereby the mission is
determined, planned, and executed.

Objections to the granting of freedom of movement for
priests, respecting all the while the needs of local churches, also
betray a monarchical understanding of ecclesiastical authority
and a noncollegial understanding of the relationship between
bishops and priests. The latter are perceived as the mere delegates and instruments of the former, to be assigned and trans-
ferred at will. The reluctance to grant men who have resigned
from the active ministry some form of ecclesiastical employment lest it upset "the simple faithful" suggests an exaggerated
understanding of the "clerical state" and, correspondingly, a
paternalistic attitude toward the nonordained membership of
the Church. Resistance to alternate forms of community (e.g.,
"floating parishes") shows an ignorance of ecclesiastical law,
and resistance to alternate forms of ministerial leadership (e.g.,
team pastorates) shows again the durability of the monarchical
concept of Church: all rule must be one-man rule, or it violates
the will of Christ.

Objections to the continuing evaluation of ministerial performance, which for many Theory A priests represents the most
serious threat of all to their identity and well-being, is also based
on the view that accountability is always and only upward,
never horizontal nor downward. Thus a pastor is accountable to

his bishop, and the bishop to the Pope; but the pastor is not accountable to his people, and certainly not to his assistants, the bishop is not accountable to his priests, and the Pope is accountable to no one, except to God, and God is remarkably reticent about his evaluative judgments. If, on the other hand, ministry is a service to the Church, not a dominative power,[74] and if that service is for the sake of the mission of the whole Church, then the membership of the Church, who are themselves responsible for the effectiveness of its mission, have a right, even a duty, to demand and to secure the best possible service they can, and to satisfy themselves at regular intervals that the quality of service they accepted at the beginning is still being delivered here and now.

Opposition to the elimination of obligatory celibacy springs from many different theological assumptions, not the least important of which are assumptions about the nature of human sexuality. Sociologically, celibacy functions as a very strong control mechanism. The dependency of the celibate group upon the organization in question is nearly total: economic, social, and emotional. Ecclesiologically, the pro-celibacy argument sees the maintenance of such control as a necessary, or at least a highly useful, instrument of organizational coherence and efficiency. The argument is wrong ecclesiologically, because the Church is not a monarchical society; and it is wrong pragmatically, because management studies have shown that efficiency and control do not go hand in hand. The way of paternalism is not efficient, even though its control is almost total.

13. ECUMENICAL RELATIONSHIPS

Objections to Catholic participation in ecumenical bodies (e.g., National Council of Churches), intercommunion, and proposals for the mutual recognition of ministries are based on the following ecclesiological assumptions: *(a)* The Catholic Church alone is the "true Church of Christ" in such wise that membership in ecumenical groups would imply that the unity these other groups are seeking does not yet exist, whereas such unity exists already in the Catholic Church. Such membership would also imply that all Christian communities are more or less equally valid expressions of the Body of Christ. *(b)* Non-Catholics do not possess a valid Eucharist, nor do they have faith in the Real Presence. Allowing Catholics to communicate at a non-Catholic service would imply acceptance of a nonexistent power; and allowing non-Catholics to communicate at a Catholic Mass would imply that faith in the Real Presence and some kind of ecclesial communion are not required for reception of the Eucharist. *(c)* Non-Catholic ministries cannot be valid because their communities are not valid expressions of the Body of Christ. Their ministries are not rooted in the apostolic ministries; non-Catholic ministries, in other words, lack the legitimacy of apostolic succession.

The first assumption cannot be reconciled with the teaching of Vatican II that, although there are "differences that exist in varying degrees between (non-Catholic Christians) and the Catholic Church," all those "who believe in Christ and have been properly baptized are brought into a certain, though imperfect, communion with the Catholic Church." They are incorporated into Christ and have a right to be honored by the title of Christian. Indeed, their communities are even called "churches."[75] Furthermore, the Theory A ecclesiology erred when it proposed that the Catholic Church can be distinguished from other Christian communities as the "one, true Church of Christ" because the Catholic Church alone possesses the marks of oneness, holiness, catholicity, and apostolicity. These marks are not possessions; they are goals. They are not to be interpreted statically, but eschatologically. The Church is called to be one, but it is not yet fully one; the Church is called to be holy, but it is clearly not yet completely holy; the Church is called to be catholic, but it does not yet embrace all truth and all values; and the Church is called to be apostolic, but it does not yet faithfully reproduce the apostolic witness, word, and service. The Church is a community of sinners, their radical grounding in the Spirit of reconciliation notwithstanding. Insofar as the Church is human and imperfect, to that same extent the Church is disunited, unholy, narrow-minded, and unfaithful. Indeed, if we accept the ecclesial reality of other Christian communities, as Vatican II has done, then it follows that the Body of Christ is larger than the Catholic Church alone. There are, however, substantial differences among the various communities within the one Body of Christ. They are divisions over doctrine, liturgy, morality, and church order. To the extent that such divisions persist, the Church cannot be called "one." Rather, the Church is always on the road to the unity which it does not yet possess. "Promoting the restoration of unity among all Christians" was, in fact, understood by the council to have been one of its chief concerns.[76] The Catholic Church, with the approval of Vatican II, has become an active participant in the ecumenical movement which the council itself defines as "those activities and enterprises which . . . are started and organized for the fostering of unity among Christians."[77] The Catholic Church certainly could not participate in a movement which is designed to foster unity if the Catholic Church were convinced that the unity already exists. It should also be pointed out that the Decree on Ecumenism does not speak of the work of unification as a "return" of non-Catholics to the Catholic Church. The council speaks rather of a "restoration" of unity. The "ecumenism-of-return" is easily endorsed by the Theory A Catholic; indeed, it is the only kind of "ecumenism" he can endorse. If that were all Vatican II was approving, it would have generated no controversy. But the council went beyond that earlier concept and spoke instead of an "ecumenism-of-restoration." The Body of Christ, of which the Catholic Church is an important, even central, part is divided. All Christians, including Catholics, must work for the restoration of ecclesial unity so that the Church may be more obviously a sign of Christ's presence in the world, a credible and effective example of *koinonia*.

The second assumption, that non-Catholics lack faith in the Real Presence and have no valid Eucharist, is contradicted by the experience of the officially approved bilateral conversations involving Catholic theologians and the theologians of other Christian traditions. In its own detailed evaluation of the consensus statements produced by these dialogues, a special committee of the Catholic Theological Society of America concluded, with approval, that the various consultations show "that Anglicans and Protestants, in many cases, do not deny, but vigorously affirm, as Roman Catholics do, the sacrificial character of the Eucharist and the real presence in the Eucharist of Christ as the living and saving Lord of the Church. This fact is not without bearing on the vexing problem of intercommunion."[78] Of all the bilateral groups, ironically it is only the Catholic-Orthodox dialogue which explicitly rejects eucharistic sharing under any circumstances today. "Ironically" because many Catholics assume that the only real differences among Christian communities is in the area of quantitative doctrinal belief. Thus the Orthodox Christians are presumably closest to Catholics because the Orthodox believe almost the same doctrines as the Catholics, with the only major difference having to do with their respective views of the papacy. And yet on the issue of intercommunion, Catholics and Orthodox are more distant from one another than are Catholics and Lutherans, Catholics and Anglicans, Catholics and Disciples of Christ, and so forth. Moreover, some form of ecclesial communion does exist, as I have already indicated in the preceding paragraph.

The third assumption, that non-Catholic ministries are invalid because they are not grounded in apostolic succession, is based on a repetition of the mechanical, chronologically oriented notion of apostolic succession to which we already referred in section 7 (see pp. 119ff). Furthermore, in the Catholic-Lutheran dialogue, which among all the consultations devoted the most attention to this problem, the Catholic theologians conclude with a statement that they "see no persuasive reason to deny the possibility of the Roman Catholic church recognizing the validity of this [Lutheran] Ministry," and they ask the authorities of the Catholic Church whether "the ecumenical urgency flowing from Christ's will for unity may not dictate" such recognition, and, correspondingly, recognition of "the presence of the body and blood of Christ in the eucharistic celebrations of the Lutheran churches."[79] The Catholic theologians argue that the New Testament evidence about who celebrated the Eucharist is sparse, that the New Testament concept of "apostle" is not univocal, and even so that there is no evidence that only an apostle or one in succession to him could celebrate. Even after the episcopal and presbyteral celebration evolved as standard practice, there were exceptions to the general rule that the only minister of the Eucharist was one ordained by a bishop. These offer some precedent for the Lutheran practice of nonepiscopal ordination. Moreover, the Catholic theologians argue, the recognition by Vatican II of the ecclesial reality of the Reformation communities, the preservation of doctrinal apostolicity in such churches as the Lutheran, and the agreement made in the joint statement on the Eucharist of both Catholics and Lutherans on the real presence and on the sacrificial nature of the Lord's Supper indicate that the difficulties which Catholics felt on these points no longer seem insuperable. The Catholic theologians note a gratifying degree of agreement with the Lutherans concerning the essentials of the ordained ministry. Specifically, Lutherans also hold the ministry to be of divine institution, that the ministry includes both preaching the word and administering the sacraments, and that there exists a distinction between the ordained ministry and the general ministry of all believers.[80]

Furthermore, if we truly acknowledge the ecclesial reality of other churches, then it follows that they must have some responsibility for the mission of the whole Church. Under ordinary circumstances, Catholics are prepared to argue, vigor-

ously, that ministry is a necessary precondition for the fulfillment of mission, indeed, that ministry is generative of the
Church itself. If we grant non-Catholic Christian communities
a share in the missionary responsibility of the Body of Christ,
how can we deny them the ministerial wherewithal to fulfill
that mission? In other words, to the extent that the non-Catholic Christian church is incorporated into the Body of Christ, to
that same extent are its various ministries valid. This represents
an exact turning-around of the usual argument: *Ubi episcopus,
ibi ecclesia* (Where the bishop is, there is the Church). Contrary
to that formula, Church is determinative of ministry, not vice
versa.[81] Walter Kasper makes a similar argument:

Mutual recognition of baptism is one of the most important elements
in the ecumenical movement. Baptism is not an isolated event. The
baptized person is incorporated into the *one* Church and his baptism
points to the Eucharist as the highest activity of the Church. The
mutual recognition of the baptism and the ecclesial character of other
churches inevitably tends towards a mutual recognition and an eventual sharing of the Eucharist. But a prior condition for the carrying out
of baptism and the Eucharist is office. This means that mutual recognition of the ecclesial character of other churches would be inconsistent
if the offices of those churches were not at the same time recognized,
although each of them has, of course, to be subjected to a detailed
theological interpretation. It is, however, simply not possible to give
with one hand what one takes away with the other.[82]

Summary

The present crisis of excessive conflict and polarization in the
Catholic Church is theologically explicable in terms of a theory-
and-practice gap. Catholics, and other Christians, hold fundamentally different views about the nature and mission of the
Church. They endorse or resist proposed changes in the institutional operations of the Church on the basis of those differing
views. On the other hand, the Church's official magisterium,
i.e., at Vatican II particularly, has articulated and disseminated

an understanding of the Church which is not the same as the ecclesiology taught and accepted in the decades preceding the council. And yet most of the present structures of the Church —its laws, disciplinary regulations, customs, administrative procedures, etc.—were created at a time when a different vision of the Church prevailed. Thus, the Church has officially moved beyond its previous self-understanding without, however, allowing its new vision to permeate and transform the given institutional apparatus. This discrepancy between theory and practice, unfortunately, is not without serious pastoral consequences. It gives rise to growing tensions, frustrations, and even schismatic tendencies. The Church cannot long sustain this kind of excessive internal conflict. Indeed, the persistence of this conflict is at the root of the present malaise of Catholic life and practice. It is a matter of utmost pastoral urgency, therefore, that the Church brings its institutional expressions into conformity with its theological perceptions. The various proposals offered in this chapter, by way of an agenda for reform, are designed for the reconciliation of theory and practice and, ultimately, for the remaking of the Church in our time.

CHAPTER IV

The Future of the Church

THE SECOND VATICAN COUNCIL identified one of the "signs of the times" as the broadening of man's dominion over time itself: "over the past by means of historical knowledge; over the future by the art of projecting and planning."[1] We have just passed through a brief period when preoccupation with "the future" has been intense: Herman Kahn's Hudson Institute studies about the year 2000;[2] Alvin Toffler's diagnosis of our collective "future shock";[3] Jürgen Moltmann's promotion of a "theology of hope."[4] Someone even published a book called *The Future of the Future.*[5]

Although popular interest seems to have edged back from the future to the present, with the newer (but similarly trendy) emphases on celebration and play, on the one hand, and on the occult and the demonic, on the other, the fundamental, future-oriented issues are still with us. The future remains a problem for theology, because the very existence and meaning of the Christian mission is conditioned by the reality of the Kingdom of God, which is the absolute future of mankind and of the world.[6] Moreover, the Kingdom of God is the destiny, not only of the Church, but of the whole of human history. For all creation in the meantime is groaning in travail, waiting to be set free from its bondage to decay and to obtain the glorious liberty of the children of God (Rom. 8:21–22). All shall see "a new heaven and a new earth" wherein God "will wipe away every tear from their eyes, and death shall be no more, neither shall there be mourning nor crying nor pain any more, for the former things (will) have passed away," and the Lord, sitting upon his throne of glory will say, "Behold, I make all things new" (Rev. 21:1, 4–5).

The Absolute and Ultimate Future of the Church

The Church's distinctive and permanent mission is to keep alive, by word and sacrament, the memory of Jesus Christ through whom God continues to reconcile all things to himself (2 Cor. 5:19); to offer itself as a kind of "first fruits" of the final heavenly feasting (James 1:18); and to do what it can, here and now, to facilitate the inbreaking of that mighty, healing power of the Spirit of the risen Lord (1 Cor. 12:1–11). That mission is distinctive because the Church alone acknowledges Jesus Christ as the lynchpin of the Kingdom; and that mission is permanent because the Kingdom in whose service the Church places itself is the final and absolute future of the world.

Indeed, the world is called to become the Kingdom of God, not to become the Church. Insofar as the Church is already the embodiment of fellowship (*koinonia*), it serves as an anticipatory sign for the rest of the world of that final, perfect community, which is the Kingdom. But signs are always temporary and provisional. When the reality they signify is immediately and directly experienced, the sign is no longer required. When the Kingdom comes in all its fullness at the end, the sacrament of that Kingdom will yield its specific identity and merge with the rest of mankind in the enjoyment of that eternal banquet of the Lord. In that sense, there is no ultimate future for the Church. Its destiny is to disappear.

To speak, therefore, about the future of the Church one must distinguish between its absolute and ultimate future, on the one hand, and its relative and proximate future, on the other.[7] The future of the Church in the absolute and ultimate sense is no different from the future of the world itself: the Kingdom of God. The Church will be given the Kingdom, however, not because it is the Church, but because it is a faithful portion of the world. No Christian, therefore, can be radically cynical about, or without hope for, the future—the overwhelming evidence of human apathy notwithstanding. The coming of the Kingdom of God does not depend intrinsically upon the achievements of mankind. The Kingdom of God is the Kingdom of *God*. It is the work of God's right hand of power, not man's (Rev. 21:1–5; Mark 11:2; Ps. 117:16).[8] It comes, not by planning and projections, but like a thief in the night (Matt. 24:42–44). In that sense at least, the Church does not, and cannot, control its own future. One may not speak, even in Teilhard's name, of the world's and the Church's progress toward the final Kingdom as if it were on an inevitably cumulative and upward-moving course, so that on the hypothetical day-before-the-last-day the world and the Church would be closest to the Kingdom's perfection. On that day of "infinity-minus-one" the world and the Church might conceivably be in the worst condition ever, in all of human and ecclesiastical history.

This absolute future of the world and of the Church is an object of hope. Every time the Church gathers for its Eucharist, it ritualizes this hope, by eating the bread and sharing the cup of the Lord, until he comes (1 Cor. 11:26). The rest of mankind, meanwhile, is "aroused to a lively hope" to the extent that other men and women, and particularly those who belong to the Church, "witness to the truth (and) share with (them) the mystery of the heavenly Father's love."[9] Thus, while the Church can, in one sense, do nothing at all to ensure the coming of that final Kingdom, it nevertheless offers itself as a credible foretaste of that future Kingdom and provides, by its own example of fidelity to the gospel, some fragile basis for holding fast to the faith and the hope that is in us.

The proposals and theological reflections contained in this book have been concerned, it should be clear, not with the absolute future of the Church, but with its relative and proximate future. It is on the basis of the Church's preparation for, and response to, the challenges of this proximate and relative future that she will be judged. For it is also the conviction of the Church that what God accomplishes through her in the present and penultimate stages of human history is "of vital concern" to that finally and absolutely future Kingdom. Indeed, "all the good fruits of our nature and enterprise"—the values of human dignity, brotherhood, freedom, etc.—will be restored to us, "but freed of stain, burnished and transfigured."[10] That final Kingdom is "already present in mystery" and it will be "brought to full flower" when the Lord returns.[11] The absolute future has even now begun.

In summary, the Church is constantly held to travel the path of renewal, self-criticism, and reform because it is called to be a sign and instrument of the Kingdom of God, which, although not yet finally realized, is already in process of realization here on earth.[12] In an unreformed state (whether through tenacity or elasticity) the Church is neither credible nor effective in its life and mission. It is for the sake of its own absolute future, and the world's, that the Church is summoned, again and again, to the way of change, of spiritual and institutional renovation. And it is on the ground of its hope in that absolute future that the Church must have the courage, even the zestful determination, to pursue that way of transformation.

The Relative and Proximate Future of the Church

Is there a point any longer to making proposals for institutional change within an organization whose long-term viability has been placed in fundamental question? Does the Church have a future (in the relative and proximate sense), and, if it does, what kind of future will it be?

How one determines the relative and proximate future of any program, agency, or movement with some degree of precision is the concern of planners, social scientists, actuaries, futurologists, and speculators. The theologian is not called upon to fulfill any of these roles (although the Church does need the help of such specialists, as I have already argued in the previous chapter). He has no charism of prescience. He ought not to dabble too much in extrapolations nor in the detailed construction of reassuring or horrifying scenarios. Theology provides only the critical norms against which the community of faith measures its word, its witness, and its service, taken in their fullest historical context. The Church cannot hope to understand its present experience if it has no sense of its own tradition. Theology seeks to clarify and sharpen the community's understanding of that tradition. But neither can the Church effectively prepare for the coming of the Kingdom of God in the future unless it takes into account the short and the long-range repercussions of its present attitudes, policies, and practices. The theologian must probe into those attitudes, policies, and practices in order to discern the theoretical assumptions underlying them, and, where necessary, to challenge and alter those assumptions, lest they continue to compromise and damage the Church's mission in the world, now and for the future. Such have, in fact, been the purpose and method of this book.

Nevertheless, even the theologian must clearly and realistically distinguish between the relative and proximate future which the Church should hope for, and the relative and proximate future which the Church might have to settle for. The proposals advanced in the third chapter are an outline of a hoped-for future. They have been submitted with the conviction that the Church has already entered one of the most critical periods in all of its history. How the Church responds to the enormous pressures of its social, political, economic, and cultural environments will very likely determine the nature and character of the Church for generations, even centuries, to come. I do not want to dramatize the crisis beyond reasonable limits, nor to imply that the situation is entirely without precedent. But history shows that the Church does not always make the right choices (as, for example, at the time of the conciliarist controversy *before* the Protestant Reformation, or during the

Modernist crisis at the beginning of this century and *before* the current period of dislocation), and that the burden of its judgmental error is usually carried by Christians far removed from the original scene. As Brian Tierney has written:

> The decrees of Constance were an attempt to give the church a juridical structure that would be in accordance with its intrinsic collegial nature. In modern times the doctrine of collegiality has been defined for us afresh; but the problem of juridical structure still remains. The Council of Constance failed and its results of that failure were disastrous for the church. We have another chance and we have less excuse for failing. We have not forgotten our history and we are not condemned to repeat it.[13]

There are many Catholics, and not a few cardinals and bishops, who would like very much to hold the line (the way of tenacity), just as there are some other Catholics—no cardinal or bishop comes to mind—who would like very much to see the Church die a slow death (the way of destruction) or arbitrarily adapt her beliefs and structures to the shifting winds, thereby retaining some semblance of modernity and attractiveness (the way of elasticity). The judgments of both extremes are based on a poor theology of the Church, a distorted understanding of doctrine, a remarkably narrow view of history, a naïve perception of sociological and psychological realities, and even a weak grasp of canon law! If either extreme view should prevail over the next ten to twenty-five years (for the die will have surely been cast by then), or perhaps even over the next five years, it is difficult to see how the Church could avoid the fate of an institutionally crippled organization, a kind of ecclesiastical British Empire, retaining its name, its traditions, the panoply of office, but without real power and influence. A tiny, faithful remnant, a church inside a church, might continue to exist within or alongside "official" Christianity, but no one—of left or right—can call that a future to be cherished and longed for. But it is still highly probable, at this moment, that the policies of containment and tenacity will be continued, with as much

repression and control as the leadership believes it can pru-
dently impose. The attrition process (declining Mass attendance, resignations from the ordained ministry and from religious communities) will not diminish; it will increase and
accelerate. More significantly, replenishment of resources from
below (in the under-twenty-five population) will simply not occur. Standards, for example, in seminary admissions policies,
may be lowered for a time in order to maintain an artificially
inflated force, but the lowering of standards has its price, and
even that compromise will eventually have to be abandoned as
the greater of two evils.

The gap between the relative and proximate future we hope
for and the relative and proximate future we might have to
settle for is potentially expansive indeed. I should argue, on the
basis of the theological reasoning set forth throughout this book,
that the Church really has no other ethical option than to pursue the path of thoroughgoing institutional reform. It is the only
course of action which can ensure a convergence of the future
we hope for and the future we will eventually settle for, a future
of vision and a future of fact.

What can concerned members of the Church do in the meantime? The five words of counsel we offered in the March 1972
statement of Catholic theologians from the United States,
Canada, and Europe are still appropriate:[14]

1. *Do not remain silent.* In this special situation silence is not
golden. The responsibility for speaking out rises in proportion
to an individual's actual and/or potential influence in the
Church. Thus, the silence of bishops who recognize the bank-
ruptcy of Theory A ecclesiology and practices and the relative
inadequacy even of Theory B ecclesiology and practices is no
longer justifiable in any sense. Those sympathetic to the need
for major reform cannot excuse themselves from raising their
voices on the pretext that they must somehow conserve their
strength for an imaginary "bigger battle." And stands must be
taken not only against tendencies toward petrification, but also

against tendencies toward dissolution. Criticism of the extreme right by moderate conservatives is far more effective than by moderate progressives. And criticism of the extreme left by moderate progressives is far more effective than by moderate conservatives. Perhaps there is no more unfortunate aspect of the current crisis of polarization than the silence of the moderates about the extremists on their own side of the ecclesiastical spectrum.

2. *Do something yourself.* Many great reform movements have had very modest beginnings. "St. Benedict," Karl Rahner reminds us, "did not know that he was fathering a new Western civilization when he went out with a few monks to refound monasticism on Monte Cassino."[15] The example of Ralph Nader, while not readily imitable, is nevertheless a very powerful indication of what a single, dedicated person can accomplish if he or she has the mind and the will to do it.

3. *Act together.* A single parishioner, a single religious, a single priest, a single bishop may not count for much, but five can make an impression and fifty can make a change. The Church needs associations of every kind, based on the principles of co-responsibility and subsidiarity, if serious institutional reform is to occur. However, these associations must cooperate with one another, and not become simply pressure groups advancing the narrow interests of their own membership.

4. *Seek provisional solutions.* It is not enough to discuss problems. One must act. This means applying constant pressure from below. It has worked in the past. We have vernacular in the liturgy, changes in the laws regarding mixed marriages, the approval of religious liberty, due process, and similar reforms precisely because of such pressure. In the meantime changes at the official level can be anticipated: intercommunion is already appropriate under certain circumstances; internal forum solutions to many marriage problems are still the only way to protect Christians from the humiliation of some tribunal procedures; married priests can continue to serve Christian

communities by conducting the liturgy of the Word, preaching, baptizing, teaching, spiritual direction, and so forth.

5. *Don't give up.* The greatest temptation is to conclude that the effort is useless and that it is better for one to quit than to keep on. Where there is no hope, there can be no action. Withdrawal from the Church is the only absolutely certain way of closing off the very possibility of reform. Resistance was to be expected. There has never been renewal without a struggle. What counts is never to lose sight of the absolute and final goal, which is the Kingdom of God. Indeed, the future of the Church has already begun. The absolute and ultimate future is already in our midst. The Spirit is in the Church, as the pledge of its future glory (2 Cor. 1:22; 5:5). Furthermore, the desire for reform is not restricted just to certain groups. There are many bishops, leaders of religious communities, laypersons, and pastors who approve and promote a profound transformation of church life. The Church cannot stop the world from developing, and the Church's own history is simply a part of that world's history. There is hope, finally, because of the Church's own faith in the power of the gospel of Jesus Christ which has shown itself, again and again, more powerful than all our human failures and foolishness, stronger than all our discouragements and frustrations.

In one sense, the future of the Church is in the hands of God alone (its absolute and ultimate future). In another sense, however, the future of the Church is the Church's own responsibility (its relative and proximate future). The Church's success in the latter instance is at least "of vital concern" to the former. To paraphrase the council's Pastoral Constitution: For after we have obeyed the Lord, and in his Spirit nurtured on earth the values of co-responsibility, accountability, unpretentious service, individual rights, freedom, human dignity, equal justice for all regardless of sex or race, truthfulness, fraternal love of all Christians, and indeed all the good fruits of our ecclesial nature and enterprise, we will find them again, but freed of stain, burnished and transfigured. This will be so when Christ hands over to the Father a Kingdom eternal and universal: a Kingdom of truth and life, of holiness and grace, of justice, love, and peace. On this earth that Kingdom is already present in mystery, and the Church is called upon to discern its presence and to respond to it creatively, imaginatively, and courageously. When the Lord returns, that Kingdom will be brought to its full flower. The Church is destined to be a part of that final harvest.

NOTES

Introduction

1. Alois Müller and Norbert Greinacher, "Editorial," *Concilium* 3/8 (March 1972), p. 8.
2. Yves Congar, "Renewal of the Spirit and Reform of the Institution," *Concilium* 3/8 (March 1972), p. 49.

Chapter I

1. *The Documents of Vatican II*, W. Abbott and J. Gallagher, eds. (New York: Guild, America, and Association Presses, 1966), pp. 712–13.
2. The relationship between John F. Kennedy and Pope John XXIII and between political and ecclesiastical liberalism has been noted frequently enough. Two recent commentaries are provided by Garry Wills, *Bare Ruined Choirs: Doubt, Prophecy, and Radical Religion* (Garden City, N.Y.: Doubleday, 1972) and David J. O'-Brien, *The Renewal of American Catholicism* (New York: Oxford University Press, 1972). For additional insight into the failures of pragmatic, as opposed to humanistic, liberalism—a distinction which Wills unfortunately does not make—see David Halberstam's *The Best and the Brightest* (New York: Random House, 1972). Charles E. Curran offers a similarly useful critique of the Johannine vision of social reform in his *Catholic Moral Theology in Dialogue* (Chicago: Fides, 1972), pp. 111–49.
3. Karl Barth, *Ad Limina Apostolorum: An Appraisal of Vatican II*, K. Crim, trans. (Richmond: John Knox Press, 1968), p. 73. The material was first published as an article, "Thoughts on the Second Vatican Council," in *The Ecumenical Review* 15 (July 1963), 357–67.
4. *Ibid.*, p. 75.

5. *Ibid.*, p. 77.
6. *Ibid.*, pp. 78–79.
7. Specific references to the conciliar documents on this and subsequent points will be provided in the second and third chapters.
8. Pastoral Constitution on the Church in the Modern World, n. 43.
9. "Justice in the World," para. 6. For the complete English text see *Synod of Bishops: The Ministerial Priesthood/Justice in the World* (Washington: United States Catholic Conference, 1972).
10. See Patrick Granfield, *Theologians at Work* (New York: Macmillan, 1967), p. 61.
11. For the papers and proceedings see *The Culture of Unbelief*, R. Caporale and A. Grumelli, eds. (Berkeley: University of California Press, 1971).
12. *Ibid.*, p. viii.
13. Dogmatic Constitution on the Church, n. 5.
14. For a fuller discussion of the relationship between the Church and the Kingdom of God, and between the Church and salvation, see my *Do We Need the Church?* (New York: Harper & Row, 1969).
15. See Hans Küng, *Infallible? An Inquiry,* E. Quinn, trans. (Garden City, N.Y.: Doubleday, 1971); *The Infallibility Debate,* John Kirvan, ed. (New York: Paulist Press, 1971); and *Mysterium Ecclesiae,* a declaration of the Vatican's Sacred Congregation for the Doctrine of the Faith (June 24, 1973). The compete text is available in *National Catholic Reporter* 9/22 (July 20, 1973), pp. 19-20. My own comment on the document is published in the same issue of *NCR*, p. 21.
16. See "Against Discouragement in the Church," a statement by thirty-four Catholic theologians from Europe and North America, *National Catholic Reporter* 8/22 (March 31, 1972), pp. 8 and 17. The reply by Cardinal Gabriele Garrone, director of the Vatican Congregation for Catholic Education, merely proved the point of the theologians' criticism; namely, that the hierarchy regards itself as having the sole responsibility for the mission of the Church. Thus Garrone accused the theologians of having "a good dose of presumption to think that they are the authentic witnesses of the Gospel, against those responsible for the Faith." (The full English text of the Garrone reply is reprinted in *The Pilot* [Boston] 143/19, [May 6, 1972], p. 8.)
17. Mike Gravel, *Citizen Power: A People's Platform* (New York: Holt, Rinehart and Winston, 1972), p. ix.

Chapter II

1. For a sample of two divergent views, see Garry Wills, *op. cit.*, and James Hitchcock, *The Decline and Fall of Radical Catholicism* (New York: Herder & Herder, 1971).
2. Peter Berger, *The Precarious Vision: A Sociologist Looks at Social Fictions and Christian Faith* (Garden City, N.Y.: Doubleday, 1961), p. 125.
3. *Sacrae Theologicae Summa* (5th ed.; Madrid: Biblioteca de Autores Cristianos, 1962). See Vol. I: *Introductio in Theologiam. De revelatione christiana. De Ecclesia Christi. De sacra Scriptura*, pp. 488–976.
4. *Ibid.*, pp. 651–53.
5. *Ibid.*, pp. 704–13.
6. *Ibid.*, pp. 815–27.
7. *Ibid.*, pp. 850–72
8. *Ibid.*, pp. 891–953.
9. Pastoral Constitution on the Church in the Modern World, n. 43.
10. Father Feeney had merely drawn the preconciliar ecclesiology to its logical conclusion, insisting that if salvation is possible only within the Roman Catholic Church, then those outside the Church are necessarily damned. The Holy Office, in its letter of August 9, 1949, to Cardinal Richard Cushing, then Archbishop of Boston, proposed a distinction between *in re* and *in voto* membership: "To gain eternal salvation it is not always required that a person be incorporated *in fact* as a member of the Church, but it is required that he belong to it in *desire* and *longing.*" This "desire" can even be implicit, when a man simply wishes to act in accord with the will of God. For the full English text of the Holy Office letter, see the *American Ecclesiastical Review* 77 (1952), 307–11.
11. Küng, *The Council, Reform, and Reunion*, Cecily Hastings, trans. (New York: Sheed & Ward, 1961), p. 14.
12. Congar, *Vraie et fausse réform dans l'Église* (Paris: Editions du Cerf, 1950).
13. See *Commentary on the Documents of Vatican II*, H. Vorgrimler, ed., L. Adolphus, *et al.*, trans. (New York: Herder & Herder, 1967), Vol. I, p. 109.
14. Dogmatic Constitution on the Church, n. 1.
15. *Idem.*

16. Pastoral Constitution, n. 2.
17. *Ibid.*, n. 40.
18. Dogmatic Constitution on the Church, n. 15, and the Decree on Ecumenism, n. 3.
19. Decree on Ecumenism, n. 3.
20. Dogmatic Constitution on the Church, n. 8.
21. See *ibid.*, n. 5, and the Pastoral Constitution, n. 39.
22. Constitution on the Sacred Liturgy, n. 59.
23. *Ibid.*, n. 11.
24. *Ibid.*, n. 14.
25. *Idem.*
26. *Ibid.*, n. 21.
27. Dogmatic Constitution on the Church. nn. 9–17, 30.
28. *Ibid.*, n. 10.
29. *Ibid.*, n. 22.
30. *Ibid.*, n. 27.
31. *Ibid.*, n. 22.
32. *Ibid.*, n. 23.
33. *Ibid.*, n. 26.
34. *Ibid.*, n. 28.
35. *Ibid.*, n. 30.
36. *Idem.*
37. *Ibid.*, n. 33.
38. Pastoral Constitution, n. 29.
39. Decree on the Apostolate of the Laity, n. 9.
40. Pastoral Constitution, n. 60.
41. Dogmatic Constitution on the Church, n. 40; see also nn. 11 and 42.
42. Decree on the Ministry and Life of Priests, n. 13; see also Dogmatic Constitution on the Church, n. 41.
43. Pastoral Constitution, n. 2.
44. *Ibid.*, n. 3.
45. *Idem.*
46. *Ibid.*, n. 16.
47. *Ibid.*, n. 38.
48. *Ibid.*, n. 39.
49. *Idem.*
50. *Ibid.*, n. 40.
51. *Ibid.*, n. 43.
52. *Idem.*
53. Decree on Ecumenism, n. 3; see also Dogmatic Constitution on the Church, n. 15.

54. Decree on Ecumenism, n. 3.
55. *Ibid.*, n. 4.
56. *Ibid.*, n. 9.
57. *Ibid.*, n. 11. For a more recent guideline, see the Secretariat for the Promotion of Christian Unity's directive of August 15, 1970, *Reflections and Suggestions concerning Ecumenical Dialogue* (Washington: United States Catholic Conference, 1970), n. IV, para. 4.
58. *Ibid.*, n. 12.
59. *Ibid.*, n. 18.
60. Declaration on the Relationship of the Church to Non-Christian Religions, n. 1.
61. Pastoral Constitution, n. 21.
62. Declaration on . . . Non-Christian Religions, n. 2.
63. Declaration on Religious Freedom, nn. 2 and 9.
64. *Ibid.*, n. 2.
65. See the Dogmatic Constitution on the Church, n. 5.
66. *Ibid.*, n. 8.
67. Pastoral Constitution, n. 45.
68. Dogmatic Constitution on the Church, n. 5.
69. *Ibid.*, n. 39.
70. For a sample of the former view, see William F. Buckley, Jr., "The Non-Latin Mass," *Commonweal* 87 (November 10, 1967), 167–69; and for the latter view, see John B. Mannion, "The Making of a Dissident," *Commonweal* 97 (January 19, 1973), 344–46.
71. The first authorized Latin-English Mass, based on the new liturgy, was celebrated at the eastern regional convention of Catholics United for the Faith, in Hartford, Conn. For a report on this meeting, see *The Catholic Transcript* (October 27, 1972), p. 2.
72. See Edward O'Connor, *The Pentecostal Movement in the Catholic Church* (Notre Dame: Ave Maria Press, 1971).
73. Charles Davis, *A Question of Conscience* (New York: Harper & Row, 1967), p. 64.
74. The full text is in the *National Catholic Reporter*, March 31, 1972, pp. 8 and 17.
75. See "Religion," *Time* 99/8 (February 21, 1972), p. 79.
76. See the *National Catholic Reporter* 9/12 (January 19, 1973), p. 5.
77. Rahner, *The Christian of the Future*, W. J. O'Hara, trans. (New York: Herder & Herder, 1967), pp. 100–1.
78. Dogmatic Constitution on the Church, n. 14.
79. *Ibid.*, n. 25, and the "Prefatory Note of Explanation," *The Documents of Vatican II*, pp. 97–101.
80. *Ibid.*, n. 14.

81. Pastoral Constitution, n. 42.

82. "Co-Responsibility: Dominating Idea of the Council and its Pastoral Consequences," in *Theology of Renewal*, L. K. Shook, ed. (New York: Herder & Herder, 1968), Vol. II, p. 11. For a further elaboration of Cardinal Suenens' views on the major issues facing the Church today, see José de Broucker, *The Suenens Dossier: The Case for Collegiality* (Notre Dame: Fides, 1970), especially pp. 7–77. The whole volume effectively supports those views, on theological and historical grounds. See, for example, Philippe Muraille, "The Logic of Vatican Council II," pp. 114–40; Gustave Thils, "Primacy and Collegiality," pp. 141–59; Roger Aubert, "Church Institutions: A Critical Interpretation," pp. 160–201; and Philippe Delhaye, "Legalism and Christian Life," pp. 202–14.

83. *Op. cit.*, p. 99.

84. Congar, "Renewal of the Spirit and Reform of the Institution," *Concilium* 3/8 (March 1972), p. 45.

85. For a useful comparative study of the different theoretical models of Church currently operative in Christian theology, see Avery Dulles, "The Church, the Churches, and the Catholic Church," *Theological Studies* 33 (June 1972), 199–234.

Chapter III

1. "Canonical Reflections on Priestly Life and Ministry," *American Ecclesiastical Review* 166 (June 1972), p. 366.

2. *The Catholic Priest in the United States: Sociological Investigations* (Washington: United States Catholic Conference, 1972), p. 312.

3. I am indebted here, at times almost literally, to the article, "The Structure and Function of Organizations," by J. Feibleman and J. W. Friend, which originally appeared in *Philosophical Review* 54 (1945), 19–44, and is reprinted in *Systems Thinking*, F. E. Emery, ed. (Hammondsworth: Penguin Books, 1969), pp. 30–55.

4. See, for example, James T. Burtchaell, *Catholic Theories of Biblical Inspiration since 1810* (Cambridge: University Press, 1969).

5. See the Pastoral Constitution on the Church in the Modern World, nn. 1–10, 45.

6. *Ibid.*, n. 10.

7. For a fuller theological development of the Church-Kingdom relationship, see two of my earlier books, *Do We Need the Church?*

(New York: Harper & Row, 1969), and *Church: the Continuing Quest* (New York: Newman Press, 1970).

8. See, for example, H. Küng, *The Church*, Ray and Rosaleen Ockenden, trans. (New York: Sheed & Ward, 1967); and Rudolf Schnackenburg, *The Church in the New Testament*, W. J. O'Hara, trans. (New York: Herder & Herder, 1965).

9. See the Pastoral Constitution, n. 4, and also the Dogmatic Constitution on the Church, Chap. II.

10. For material in this section I am relying upon the collected studies, *Management and Motivation*, V. H. Vroom and E. L. Deci, eds. (Hammondsworth: Penguin Books, 1970).

11. See "Employee Attitudes and Employee Performance," by A. H. Brayfield and W. H. Crockett, *Psychological Bulletin* 52 (1955), 396–424. An excerpt of the article is reprinted in *Management and Motivation*, pp. 72–82.

12. See Maslow, "A Theory of Human Motivation," *Psychological Review* 50 (1943), 370–396. An abridged version of that article is reprinted in *Management and Motivation*, pp. 27–41.

13. See V. Vroom and E. Deci, "Introduction: An Overview of Work Motivation," *Management and Motivation*, pp. 9–19.

14. See Greeley, *The Catholic Priest in the United States*, p. 312.

15. Maslow, "A Theory of Human Motivation," *op. cit.*; see also his *Eupsychian Management: A Journal* (Homewood, Ill.: Irwin-Dorsey, 1965). This kind of management is on the whole impossible "where fear reigns" (p. 23).

16. See Brian Tierney, "Roots of Western Constitutionalism in the Church's Own Tradition: the Significance of the Council of Constance," in *We, the People of God . . . a Study of Constitutional Government for the Church*, James A. Coriden, ed. (Huntington, Ind.: Our Sunday Visitor Press, 1968), pp. 113–28.

17. *Ibid.*, p. 127.

18. "Towards Constitutional Development within the Church: Position Paper," *ibid.*, p. 8. See also Edward Heston, "Present Organizational Design and Structure of the Roman Catholic Church," *ibid.*, pp. 29–47, and G. Zizola, "The Reformed Roman Curia," *ibid.*, pp. 49–77.

19. See John E. Lynch, "Co-Responsibility in the First Five Centuries: Presbyteral Colleges and the Election of Bishops," in *Who Decides for the Church? Studies in Co-Responsibility*, J. A. Coriden, ed. (Hartford: Canon Law Society of America, 1971), pp. 14–53. See also William Bassett, "Subsidiarity, Order, and Freedom in the

Church," *ibid.*, pp. 205–65, and Myles Bourke, "Collegial Decision-Making in the New Testament," *ibid.*, pp. 1–13.

20. "Position Paper," *We, the People of God*, p. 9.
21. *Ibid.*, p. 14. See also Andrew Greeley, "A Social Organizational View of the Catholic Church," *ibid.*, pp. 81–89; and Donald Warwick, "Personal and Organizational Effectiveness in the Roman Catholic Church," *ibid.*, pp. 91–110.
22. While this proposal is entirely consistent with the constitutional principles set forth in *We, the People of God*, it has not yet been advanced by any professional society or group of scholars within the Catholic Church. However, a procedure for administrative review is presently being studied by the Pontifical Commission for the Revision of the Code of Canon Law (see *The Jurist* 32/2 (1972), p. 292, and *ibid.*, 32–3 (1972), 417–18). A useful model is provided by United States Senator Mike Gravel, of Alaska, in his *Citizen Power*, pp. 45–46 (see Chap. I, n. 17, above).
23. Greeley, *The Catholic Priest in the United States*, p. 321.
24. See J. E. Lynch, *op. cit., Who Decides for the Church?*, pp. 14–53; and Robert Benson, "Election by Community and Chapter: Reflections on Co-Responsibility in the Historical Church," pp. 54–80. See especially the "Statement of Consensus," *ibid.*, pp. 280–84.
25. This is true even in such relatively progressive proposals as the Canon Law Society of America's "The Plan for Choosing Bishops," which was accepted "in substance" at the society's October 1971 convention. The plan is reprinted in *Origins: NC Documentary Service* 2/1 (May 25, 1972), pp. 3 and 18. For the theological foundations, see my essay, "A Preliminary Ecclesiological Statement," in *The Choosing of Bishops: Historical and Theological Studies*, William Bassett, ed. (Hartford: Canon Law Society of America, 1971), pp. 11–20. See also John T. Finnegan, "The Present Canonical Practice in the Catholic Church," *ibid.*, pp. 85–102.
26. "Infaillibilité et indefectibilité," *Revue des sciences philosophiques et théologiques* 54 (1970), 607–8; also his *L'Église de saint Augustin à l'époque moderne* (Paris: Editions du Cerf, 1970), pp. 450–77, especially pp. 471–72.
27. One of the most recent volumes on this subject is "The Petrine Ministry in the Church," H. Küng, ed., *Concilium* 4/7 (April 1971). See especially Rudolf Pesch, "The Position and Significance of Peter in the Church of the New Testament: A Survey of Current Research," pp. 21–35; and James McCue, "Roman Primacy in the First Three Centuries," pp. 36–44. See also H. Küng, *The Church*,

pp. 444–80; *Structures of the Church*, S. Attanasio, trans. (New York: Nelson, 1964), pp. 224–394; and *Infallible? An Inquiry*. In connection with the last of the three works, see *The Infallibility Debate*, and especially my own essay which places the infallibility question in the larger context of the nature and mission of the Church, pp. 35–65 (see Chap. I, n. 15, above).

28. See *We, the People of God*, p. 15.
29. See, for example, Raymond Brown, *Priest and Bishop: Biblical Reflections* (New York: Paulist Press, 1970), Chap. II, "Are the Bishops the Successors of the Apostles?," pp. 47–86, and André Lemaire, *Les ministères aux origines de l'Église* (Paris: Editions du Cerf, 1971). See also H. Küng, *The Church* and *Structures of the Church* (n. 27, above).
30. See "Apostolic by Succession?", H. Küng, ed., *Concilium* 4/4 (April 1968), and especially H. Küng, "What is the Essence of Apostolic Succession?", pp. 16–19; Avery Dulles, "The Succession of Prophets in the Church," pp. 28–32; and Arnold van Ruler, "Is There a 'Succession of Teachers'?", pp. 33–37.
31. See M. Bourke, "Collegial Decision-Making in the New Testament," *op. cit.*, p. 13.
32. Dogmatic Constitution on the Church, n. 4.
33. "Toward a Declaration of Christian Rights: A Position Paper," in *The Case for Freedom: Human Rights in the Church*, J. A. Coriden, ed. (Washington: Corpus Books, 1969), pp. 12–14. See also *On Due Process: A Summary of Actions Taken by the National Conference of Catholic Bishops on the Subject of Due Process* (Washington: United States Catholic Conference, 1970). The plan has received papal approval (see *The Jurist* 32/2 [1972], 291–92).
34. According to Lawrence Wrenn, *officialis* (chief marriage court judge) of the archdiocese of Hartford, Conn., during 1971 marriage tribunals in the United States annulled or prepared for dissolution something less than three thousand apparently valid marriages. Perhaps twice that many people received a preliminary hearing regarding the merits of their case, so that it might be said that nine or ten thousand people had their cases reviewed by a tribunal during the year. This is not a very impressive number when one compares it with the 120,000 civil divorces that were granted during the same year from presumably valid marriages involving Catholics. See Wrenn's essay, "Marriage: Indissoluble or Fragile?" in *Divorce and Remarriage in the Catholic Church*, L. G. Wrenn, ed. (New York: Paulist Press, 1973), Chap. X.

35. *We, the People of God,* James A. Coriden, ed., pp. 12–13.
36. Resolution #7, Canon Law Society of America, 34th annual convention, Seattle, Washington, October 1972. For an in-depth study of the internal forum solution, see the entire issue of *The Jurist* 30/1 (1970).
37. See his essay, "A Theological Appraisal of Marriage Tribunals," *Divorce and Remarriage in the Catholic Church,* Chap. II.
38. Wrenn, *op. cit.*
39. "Women in the Church" (consensus statement of the Roman Catholic/Reformed Presbyterian consultation), *Journal of Ecumenical Studies* 9/1 (Winter 1972), 235–41.
40. See the report of the Catholic Theological Society of America's special study committee on the bilateral consultations, submitted to the CTSA's board of directors in July 1972, and published in the society's *Proceedings of the Twenty-Seventh Annual Convention* (New York: Manhattan College, 1973), Vol. 27, p. 205; see also the report of the subcommittee on the systematic theology of the priesthood, submitted to the National Conference of Catholic Bishops, September 1971, p. 36 (unpublished).
41. See "A Pledge of Leadership" (Conference of Major Religious Superiors of Men), *Origins* 2/7 (July 13, 1972), 112–13; see also "Women Religious/Their Life Today" (Leadership Conference of Women Religious), *Origins* 2/15 (October 5, 1972), 238–39, 245–49.
42. "What we are witnessing is not merely a disagreement between those who have power and those who do not, but a disagreement among those with opposing ideologies about the nature of the reality whose power structure is the subject of disagreement. Power conflicts that are rooted in ideological differences tend to be much more serious than power conflicts among those who share the same ideologies." (A. Greeley, *The Catholic Priest in the United States,* p. 154).
43. *Ibid.,* p. 271, *et passim.*
44. See "Canonical Reflections on Priestly Life and Ministry" (n. 1, above), pp. 363–92. This paper is the product of a canonical colloquium held at, and sponsored by, the School of Canon Law, of the Catholic University of America.
45. Circular letter on presbyteral councils, April 11, 1970. Cited in "Canonical Reflections . . . ," p. 370.
46. Richard Dillon, "Biblical Approaches to the Priesthood," *Worship* 46/8 (1972), p. 470.

47. Pastoral Constitution on the Church in the Modern World, n. 26. See the Canon Law Society of America's study, "The Future Discipline of Priestly Celibacy," *The Jurist* 32/2 (1972), 273–89.
48. See the symposium "A Round Table: Where Are We in Ecumenism?" *America* 126/3 (January 22, 1972), 50–66.
49. CTSA report on the bilateral consultations, pp. 230–31. See also the resolution which I submitted to, and which was accepted by, the CTSA's twenty-sixth annual convention in Baltimore, June 1971 (*Proceedings*, Vol. 26, p. 256).
50. See Avery Dulles' contribution to the *America* symposium, *op. cit.*, p. 55. See also "Patterns of Relationships between the Roman Catholic Church and the World Council of Churches," *The Ecumenical Review* 24/3 (July 1972), 247–88, and *Report on Possible Roman Catholic Membership in the National Council of Churches* (Washington: United States Catholic Conference, 1972).
51. See again the Dogmatic Constitution on the Church, Chaps. II and IV.
52. A very serious analysis of these tendencies is presented in Alois Grillmeier, *Christ in Christian Tradition: From the Apostolic Age to Chalcedon (451)*, J. Bowden, trans. (New York: Sheed & Ward, 1965).
53. See Karl Rahner, *The Church and the Sacraments*, W. J. O'Hara, trans. (London: Nelson, 1963); and Edward Schillebeeckx, *Christ the Sacrament of Encounter with God*, P. Barrett, *et al.*, trans. (New York: Sheed & Ward, 1963); also the Dogmatic Constitution on the Church, n. 1.
54. *The Once and Future Church: A Communion of Freedom*, J. A. Coriden, ed. (New York: Alba House, 1971), pp. 268–70. For another excellent statement, see Cardinal Leo Suenens, *Coresponsibility in the Church*, F. Martin, trans. (New York: Herder & Herder, 1968).
55. For the antimonarchical theological arguments, see Karl Rahner and Joseph Ratzinger, *The Episcopate and the Primacy*, K. Barker, *et al.*, trans. (New York: Herder & Herder, 1962), especially pp. 11–19. In an absolute monarchy, Rahner reminds us, everything within the bounds of physical possibility and morality proceeds from the will of one man, and of one man only. Clearly the Pope is not a monarch in that sense. He is limited, even constitutionally, by the existence of the episcopate. The episcopate itself is of divine right. The Pope could not abolish the office of bishop. Indeed, it is only when his office is conjoined with the episcopate that the papal

primacy constitutes the Church (pp. 15–17). See also R. Pesch, "The New Testament Foundations of a Democratic Form of Life in the Church," *Concilium* 3/7 (March 1971), 48–59.

56. J. E. Lynch, "The History of Centralization: Papal Reservations," *The Once and Future Church*, p. 57.
57. B. Tierney, *op. cit.*, *We, the People of God*, p. 127.
58. See n. 42, above.
59. See the Dogmatic Constitution on the Church, n. 8.
60. See my article, "A Preliminary Ecclesiological Statement," in *The Choosing of Bishops*, pp. 11–20.
61. See, again, *Who Decides for the Church?*: articles by M. Bourke on the New Testament experience, by J. E. Lynch on the first five centuries, and by J. T. McNeil on the conciliarist period. In *The Choosing of Bishops* see Thomas O'Meara, "Emergence and Decline of Popular Voice in the Selection of Bishops," pp. 21–32, and Robert Trisco, "The Variety of Procedures in Modern History," pp. 33–60.
62. See "Statement of Consensus," *Who Decides for the Church?*, pp. 280–84.
63. See the "Position Paper" in *The Once and Future Church*, pp. 267–70. See also my article, "Collegiality: State of the Question," *ibid.*, pp. 1–24.
64. See, for example, Karl Rahner, *The Episcopate and the Primacy*, p. 122.
65. Raymond Brown, *Priest and Bishop*, p. 73.
66. *Ibid.*, p. 74.
67. See n. 30, above.
68. Myles Bourke, "Collegial Decision-Making in the New Testament," *ibid.*, p. 13.
69. "Toward a Declaration of Christian Rights," *The Case for Freedom*, p. 8.
70. L.G. Wrenn, *op. cit.* For a thorough review of the recent literature on indissolubility, see Richard McCormick, "Notes on Moral Theology," *Theological Studies* 32 (March 1971), 107–22; and 33 (March 1972), 91–100. See also John Noonan, *The Power to Dissolve* (Cambridge, Mass.: Belknap Press, 1972).
71. John L. McKenzie, "Ministerial Structures in the New Testament," *Concilium* 4/8 (April 1972), p. 22.
72. *Idem.*
73. Pastoral Constitution on the Church in the Modern World, n. 29;

see also Karl Rahner, "Church and World," *Sacramentum Mundi,*
K. Rahner, *et al.,* eds. (New York: Herder & Herder, 1968), Vol. I,
pp. 346–57.
74. J. L. McKenzie, *Authority in the Church* (New York: Sheed &
Ward, 1966). For studies on the evaluation of ministerial performance see Felix M. Lopez, "Evaluating Priestly Performance,"
The Jurist 32/2 (1972), 234–52, and also his "Performance Evaluation for Pastors," *Canon Law Society of America: Proceedings,* Vol.
3 (Hartford: Canon Law Society of America, 1971), pp. 55–61.
75. Decree on Ecumenism, n. 3.
76. *Ibid.,* n. 1.
77. *Ibid.,* n. 4.
78. *Op. cit.,* p. 216 (see n. 40, above).
79. *Lutherans and Catholics in Dialogue, IV: Eucharist and Ministry*
(Washington: United States Catholic Conference; New York: Lutheran World Federation, 1970), p. 32.
80. *Ibid.,* pp. 23–33.
81. See John A. T. Robinson, "Kingdom, Church and Ministry," in *The
Historic Episcopate in the Fullness of the Church,* K. M. Carey, ed.
(2nd ed.; London: Dacre Press, 1960), pp. 11–22; see also my book,
The Church in the Thought of Bishop John Robinson (Philadel-
phia: Westminster Press, 1966), pp. 73–94.
82. Walter Kasper, "Convergence and Divergence in the Question of
Office," *Concilium* 4/8 (April 1972), 116–17. The whole issue is
devoted to this topic.

Chapter IV

1. Pastoral Constitution on the Church in the Modern World, n. 5.
2. H. Kahn and Anthony Wiener, *The Year 2000: A Framework for
Speculation on the Next Thirty-Three Years* (New York: Macmillan,
1967).
3. Alvin Toffler, *Future Shock* (New York: Random House, 1970).
4. Jürgen Moltmann, *Theology of Hope* (New York: Harper & Row,
1967).
5. John McHale, *The Future of the Future* (New York: Braziller,
1969).
6. See Edward Schillebeeckx, *God the Future of Man,* N. D. Smith,
trans. (New York: Sheed & Ward, 1968).

7. See Karl Rahner, "Marxist Utopia and The Christian Future of Man," *Theological Investigations*, K. and H. Kruger, trans. (Baltimore: Helicon, 1969), Vol. VI, pp. 59–68.
8. See Rudolf Schnackenburg, *God's Rule and Kingdom*, J. Murray, trans. (London: Nelson, 1963), esp. pp. 77–86.
9. Pastoral Constitution, n. 93.
10. *Ibid.*, n. 39.
11. *Idem.*
12. Dogmatic Constitution on the Church, n. 1.
13. Brian Tierney, *op. cit.*, *We, the People of God*, pp. 127–28.
14. *National Catholic Reporter* 8/22 (March 31, 1972), pp. 8 and 17.
15. Karl Rahner, "A Theological Interpretation of the Position of Christians in the Modern World," in *Mission and Grace*, Cecily Hastings, trans. (London: Sheed & Ward, 1963), Vol. I, p. 53.

GLOSSARY

Key Terms in Chapter II

Theory A: A view of the Church, commonly accepted by Catholics in the years preceding Vatican II (before 1962), which understands the Church primarily as a visible society, hierarchically structured, whose mission is the salvation of souls accomplished through the preaching of the Word and the administration of the sacraments.

Practices A: The attitudes, values, and customs of Catholics in the years preceding Vatican II based on, and validated by, Theory A, e.g., clericalized liturgy, monarchical pastoral authority, exclusion of Protestants and other non-Catholic Christians from the Body of Christ, etc.

Theory B: The view of the Church generally adopted and proposed by the Second Vatican Council, emphasizing the Church as a community (People of God) rather than as a visible society (hierarchical institution); indeed, a community which includes Protestants and other non-Catholic Christians, a community of shared responsibility, etc.

Practices B: The changes in the attitudes, values, and customs of Catholics initiated and supported by the doctrines and directives of Vatican II, e.g., the creation of parish councils, the extension of ecumenical activities, a new emphasis on the Church's social responsibilities, etc.

Theory C: A view of the Church which has been developing in the years immediately following the Second Vatican Council (1966–   ) and which is, in one sense, a refinement of Theory B; namely, Theory C strips Theory B of the residue of preconciliar ecclesiology (Theory A) and italicizes those elements of the conciliar teaching which represent a correction of the preconciliar view of the Church.

Practices C: The changes in attitudes, values, and customs which are, or eventually will be, prompted by certain key principles contained in the conciliar documents and in the work of contemporary ecclesiastical scholarship, e.g., the selection of bishops by a more representative and public process, the conferral of deliberative (policy-making) power on parish councils, mutual recognition of ordained ministries, etc. (see the Agenda for Reform in Chapter III).

Key Terms in Chapter III

A. ON INSTITUTIONAL RESPONSE TO CHANGE

1. *The way of tenacity:* Like the rock, an institution refuses either to give to, or to interact with, its environment. It is a matter of "holding the line." The possibility of growth is sacrificed for the sake of survival.
2. *The way of elasticity:* Like the kelp, an institution simply moves and sways with the changes dictated by its environment. It is a matter of "bending with the times," but not on the basis of any fixed principles. The possibility of real growth here, too, is sacrificed for the sake of survival.
3. *The way of self-determination:* Like the porpoise, an institution, no longer preoccupied with survival alone, willingly takes risks, invests in its environment, and engages in a give-and-take, but without compromise of its institutional goals and integrity. It is a matter of being responsive to the "signs of the times" in order to realize more effectively the institution's purposes.

B. ON MOTIVATING PEOPLE FOR CHANGE

1. *The way of paternalism:* This method assumes that people who are satisfied with their job will more likely be effective at that job. The greater the rewards, the more productive the worker. The motivation is essentially one of gratitude and loyalty.
2. *The way of scientific management:* This method assumes that a person will be motivated to work if rewards *and penalties* are attached directly to his *performance.* Unlike the way of paternalism, rewards are conditional, not unconditional. Motivationally this method is based on the principle of reinforcement, i.e., if a person undertakes an action and this action is followed by a reward (penalty), the probability is that the action will be repeated (eliminated).
3. *The way of participative management:* This method assumes that individuals can derive satisfaction from doing an effective job per se. Motivation is twofold: *(a)* the worker perceives a connection between the goals of the organization and his own personal goals; and *(b)* by participating in the decision-making process, the worker feels a sense of personal responsibility for the outcome of the project in question.

INDEX

Index of Names

Index of Subjects